D0945284

ERNEST HEMINGWAY
The Papers of a Writer

ERNEST HEMINGWAY
The Papers of a Writer

Edited, with an introduction, by
Bernard Oldsey

GARLAND PUBLISHING, INC. • NEW YORK & LONDON
1981

Published by Garland Publishing, Inc. in cooperation with
West Chester State College and the John F. Kennedy Library

Library of Congress Cataloging in Publication Data

Main entry under title:

Ernest Hemingway, the papers of a writer.

  Proceedings of a conference held in July 1980
on Thompson's Island, Boston Harbor.
    1. Hemingway, Ernest, 1899–1961—Congresses.
2. Hemingway, Ernest, 1899–1961—Archives—
Congresses. 3. Authors, American—20th century—
Biography—Congresses. I. Oldsey, Bernard Stanley,
1923–
PS3515.E37Z5869   813'.52   80-9031
ISBN 0-8240-9303-8   AACR2

Printed on acid-free, 250-year-life paper
Manufactured in the United States of America

This book is dedicated to Mary Welsh Hemingway
who was unable, because of illness, to attend
the conference that she herself made possible.

CONTENTS

ILLUSTRATIONS

ACKNOWLEDGMENTS

In addition to my fellow contributors, whose names can be found in the table of contents, I wish to thank the following persons for their help and cooperation: Dan H. Fenn, Director of the Kennedy Library, and those members of his staff who made the Hemingway Conference in Boston possible; President Charles G. Mayo and Provost Richard G. Branton of West Chester State College, who cut through red-tape to make this book possible; Charles Scribner, Jr., who provided moral support for the conference and permission for quotation from the published works of Ernest Hemingway; and Anita Eggert, who provided aid in the many tasks associated with the editing and preparation of manuscript.

INTRODUCTION

Perhaps even the lesser gods of public taste and common mores also see the truth but wait. At least this seems to be the case with Ernest Hemingway. When his *A Farewell to Arms* was published in October of 1929, it was immediately banned in Boston as an immoral work. A little over a half-century later, however, in July of 1980, the Hemingway Room was officially opened at the John F. Kennedy Library in Boston. The Library now contains not only numerous copies of *A Farewell to Arms* (in various editions, languages, and pre-publication forms) but also the great bulk of the author's literary effects, including correspondence, notes, manuscripts, typescripts, photographs, and printer's proofs.

This modern instance of "O tempora, O mores" is to a considerable extent responsible for the publication of this present collection of essays. Each of the essays had its own generative spark, but the collection as a whole can be traced back to a series of letters written by Jo August, Curator of the Hemingway Collection at the Kennedy Library. In the fall of 1979, she wrote to a dozen scholars who had had opportunity to work with the Hemingway papers, either while they were still being gathered together by Mary Hemingway, or later when they were deposited in the Library's temporary quarters at Waltham, Massachusetts. After more than a decade at Waltham, all of the Library's holdings were in the process of being transferred to the permanent site at Columbia Point. The new federal building erected there (a magnificent ship-like structure designed by I.M. Pei) had just been dedicated, with President Jimmy Carter and Senator Edward Kennedy officiating. At this time, Jo August sought some appropriate means of commemorating the dedication of the special Hemingway Room. One of her letters, dated 14 September 1979, runs in part as follows:

> Dear _____ ,
> . . . tell me. Would you be interested in giving, chairing, sharing a session on "Beginnings and Endings" or something in the middle, at "Papers of a Writer," a conference to celebrate the dedication of the Hemingway Room at the Kennedy Library? The conference will take place at Thompson's Island in Boston Harbor. . . .

As this book indicates, the conference did take place—in July of 1980, during one of the most sweltering periods in the history of Boston; and on Thompson's Island, a lovely place, but one unrelieved by electric fans or air conditioning, and untouched by cooling sea breezes during the period mentioned. Nonetheless, as all of those who attended agreed, July was the right time for the conference: Ernest Hemingway was born on July 21, 1899; was first wounded on July 8, 1918; and died on July 2, 1961. It seemed absolutely fitting, then, that the Hemingway Room would be officially opened (with Patrick Hemingway and Jacqueline Kennedy Onassis cutting the symbolic ribbon) on July 18, 1980; and that on the very same day, under a shade tree on nearby Thompson's Island, the Hemingway Society would be born.

These activities signaled something of a new beginning. Nineteen years after his death, the papers of Ernest Hemingway were now, most of them, housed in one convenient place and about to be made much more open to scholarly and critical investigation and assessment. Establishment of the Hemingway Society indicated the increased need for cooperation among those undertaking such tasks. The very act of opening the Hemingway Room raised the kind of bibliographical, biographical, and critical questions one would naturally expect when the papers of any great writer have been made accessible—

Of what, for example, do the papers actually consist? Where have they been gathered from? How did they come to be placed in this particular repository? How have they been arranged, codified? In a larger sense, what do they tell about the life and times of the author that we did not previously know? What new publications will they give rise to? What can they tell about the author's method of composition, his method of selectivity, his subsumed and yet contributory thematic and artistic impulses? How can these papers help in our better understanding and appreciation of the published works? To what extent will they rectify or reinforce our readings of the canon, or our overall critical estimation of the author?

The essays that make up this book reflect all of these questions and provide some of the answers. The essays are based on presentations made at the commemorative conference; they have been changed in various respects to meet the demands of print and a wider audience than that group of specialists (nearly a hundred scholars from Canada, France, and Jugoslavia, as well as the U.S.) who gathered together on Thompson's Island, and later joined approximately two hundred other celebrants at the Kennedy Library festivities.

Jo August, in the opening note of the book, provides a capsule account of what the Hemingway Collection includes and how the material was brought together finally in such a clean, well-lighted repository. George Plimpton, in his "JFK and Hemingway," explains how these two titular men, both practiced in the art of profiling courage, have become associated after their deaths; and why the Hemingway Collection ended up in Boston (a city the author had never even visited) instead of Oak Park, Key West, or Ketchum. Correspondingly, James D. Brasch and Joseph

Sigman, in their account of "Hemingway's Library," indicate how a number of the author's literary possessions still remain in the Finca Vigia, his former residence outside Havana. And Jacqueline Tavernier-Courbin, in "The Mystery of the Ritz Hotel Papers," investigates the question of where certain of Hemingway's papers had been stored, and how they may have been gathered from places as distant as Paris.

Of course, the story of the Hemingway Collection is mainly the story of Mary Hemingway and the manner in which she has managed her husband's literary effects. Few who have observed her activities over the past two decades can doubt her ability as literary executor. She has acted as sometime editor (in bringing out *A Moveable Feast*, in 1964; and *Islands in the Stream*, with the aid of Charles Scribner, Jr., in 1970) and as full-time guardian, exercising considerable taste and judgment in permitting reputable scholars to utilize Hemingway's correspondence and manuscripts in their endeavors. Moreover, her autobiographic *How It Was*, 1976, probably ranks second only to Carlos Baker's authorized biography in providing specific information about Hemingway the man. Much of the attitude that has guided her in managing the papers is, incidentally, revealed in the autobiography. Commenting on her rejection of Malcolm Cowley's well-intentioned suggestion that the papers be turned over to a committee of worthy scholars, she declares that "A more careless or conscientious widow might have said yes," and at the same time admits that continuing to work with her husband's papers has "given point and purpose to my days."

Her stewardship also gave point and purpose to the days of others, including Carlos Baker, who had early access to the papers in writing *Ernest Hemingway: A Life Story* (1969), and who used them again in editing *Ernest Hemingway: Selected Letters, 1917–1961* (1981). Much the same can be said of Philip Young, who had a hand in arranging and editing *The Nick Adams Stories* (1972), and who, along with Charles W. Mann, produced *The Hemingway Manuscripts: An Inventory* (1969), a pioneer codification of the manuscripts.

There have been others who have benefited from Mary Hemingway's permission to examine, and in certain instances publish, sections of the Hemingway papers. On this basis, Michael Reynolds published *Hemingway's First War* in 1976 and Bernard Oldsey his *Hemingway's Hidden Craft* in 1979. These turned out to be companion volumes on the methods of composition employed in the making of *A Farewell to Arms*, and they are indicative of the kind of work that has been accomplished since the papers began accumulating in the Kennedy Library. Along with the essays included here in *Ernest Hemingway: The Papers of a Writer*, these works indicate the direction that Hemingway studies will take in the future. One fact emerging from the Thompson's Island conference is that all previous Hemingway commentary will have to be re-examined in the light of new evidence available in the papers. Another fact—something of a corollary—is that all new commentary will have to be guided by this evidence.

These facts are apparent in E.R. Hagemann's examination of letters from "Hemingway's Early Years." Previously unavailable, these documents clarify a number of points about Hemingway's familial relations and, more important, the influence Ezra Pound exerted on his early career. Likewise, Scott Donaldson's essay on "Hemingway of *The Star*" adds much to our understanding of how the young writer struggled with the dictates of journalism and then began transcending them to meet the demands of fiction. Working with newly available correspondence and journalistic pieces as yet unpublished, Donaldson goes considerably beyond what we knew from such previous works as Charles Fenton's *The Apprenticeship of Ernest Hemingway* (1954) and *By-Line: Ernest Hemingway*, edited by William White (1967).

Two other essays appearing here, both stressing European sources, clarify influences exerted on Hemingway. The first is "Hemingway's Poetry: Angry Notes of an Ambivalent Overman," by Nicholas Gerogiannis, editor of *88 Poems* [Ernest Hemingway], published in 1980. Through Hemingway's verse and *Across the River and Into the Trees*, Gerogiannis traces elements of superman-ism deriving in part from Friedrich Nietzsche, but mainly from the fiction and pronunciamentos of Gabriele D'Annunzio. The second influence essay is Zvonimir Radeljković's "Initial Europe." Here Radeljković uses manuscript material from two unpublished short stories of Hemingway's to demonstrate the effect Europe had on the shaping of his early *Weltanschauung*.

Along narrower social lines, Linda W. Wagner's essay on "Women in Hemingway's Early Fiction" utilizes manuscript material to support a contention that a shift occurred in Hemingway's emphasis on, and his treatment of, female characters—a shift from sensitive awareness to harshness to eventual deemphasis. In still another vein, employing manuscript variants from three vital stories ("Indian Camp," "Big Two-Hearted River," and "The Short Happy Life of Francis Macomber"), Bernard Oldsey investigates the ways in which Hemingway worked on the "Beginnings and Endings" of his fiction. It is in this respect that the papers appear to be most revealing about Hemingway's craft as a writer and skill as a self-editor.

All of these forms of investigation are discussed by Michael Reynolds in his analysis of "The Next Ten Years of Hemingway Studies." With clarity and force, Reynolds provides extrapolative signposts for the future and sets up some necessary lines of communication and demarcation. This is a remarkably politic and prescient assessment of matters, and it is nicely balanced by the final piece in the book, written by Philip Young. (It should be noted here that with the exception of George Plimpton's contribution—a postprandial talk at the dedication ceremonies at the Kennedy Library—the essays in this book follow their order of presentation at the conference on "The Papers of a Writer.")

Young's "Occasional Remarks" contain some cogent and sobering thoughts about "Hemingway Studies" and what such a phrase might betoken. He casts a backward glance over the critical road taken during the past half-century—from the time when non-academicians, like Edmund Wilson and Malcolm Cowley, first began to provide commentary on Hemingway, to the present when something like a Hemingway "industry," with headquarters in academe, has begun to threaten the ecology of both "Big Two-Hearted River" and "The Territory Ahead."

Between Reynolds and Young, between the covers of this book, there exist two truths about the study of Ernest Hemingway; namely, the truth of organization and cooperation, and the truth of individual critical analysis and perception. It is fair to say that the contributions of Edmund Wilson, Malcolm Cowley, Carlos Baker, Philip Young, Earl Rovit, and Arthur Waldhorn will stand for a long time. No one working on Hemingway in the future will ignore the essential contributions made by these and a number of other critics, like Jackson Benson. It is also fair to say, however, that these earlier works will have to be checked—and in many instances added to and emended—because of the information contained in the papers.

The papers, so far as can be seen, contain no great shockers. They provide no evidence that Hemingway was a closet homosexual, or any other kind. They do not show that he was abnormally attracted to his mother or sisters. They do not contain any unpublished great novels or short stories. But they do contain hundreds, thousands of pieces of information that are going to lead to a fine biography (one which will depend basically on Baker's and then round matters off). They also contain clues to corrected, refined, and perhaps substantially new critical statements about the canonical works—in respect to how they were written, and how they can be read in the light of conflated texts. All who would rival those having thus far done the best critical work on Hemingway will have to make full use of the papers, performing the duties of investigative scholarship. At the same time, however, they will have to keep before them an obvious but guiding dictum: The proper study of a writer is his writing; everything else is simply contributory.

Bernard Oldsey
West Chester, Pa.
December 30, 1980

The John F. Kennedy Library, at Columbia Point, Boston, Mass.

The official opening of the Hemingway Room, JFK Library: Jacqueline Kennedy Onassis; Patrick Hemingway; Dan H. Fenn, Director of the Library; William W. Moss, Chief Archivist. Date: July 18, 1980.

A section of the Hemingway Room, JFK Library.

Ernest Hemingway in his library at the Finca Vigia.

A NOTE ON THE HEMINGWAY COLLECTION

For three days on a seemingly tropical island in Boston Harbor, a group of Hemingway enthusiasts and scholars gathered to talk about the papers of a writer. The conferees knew they had come to celebrate the official opening of the Hemingway Room at the John F. Kennedy Library, the dedication of a new, comfortable, and congenial center for Hemingway studies. But there was another private celebration going on at the same time, a celebration of the virtual completion of the organization and description of the Hemingway Collection.

Mary Hemingway started depositing papers in the Library in 1972. The first materials to arrive were about two feet of miscellaneous and fragmentary manuscripts. From that point until 1980, papers continued to arrive at the Library. There were materials from Mary Hemingway's New York apartment, her home in Ketchum, from Harvard's Houghton Library, and from Carlos Baker in Princeton. The bulk of the collection, however, came from two sources: Mary Hemingway's bank vault in New York, the contents of which Charles Mann and Philip Young listed in their Inventory, and from warehouse storage in New York. The papers arrived in boxes, trunks, filing cabinets, and shopping bags. For the most part they were not organized, and the first task was gross sorting by type: manuscripts, correspondence, photographs, publications, and other. All manuscript materials were sent to the New England Document Conservation Center, where they were deacidified, and then repaired, separated, cleaned, and mylar encapsulated as necessary. Intensive preservation work was performed on the five very fragile scrapbooks kept by Grace Hall Hemingway from Ernest's birth until he was 18 years of age. The newspaper clipping scrapbooks were taken apart and the clippings were deacidified and encapsulated. Copy negatives were made of the over 10,000 still photographs, and the materials were placed in acid-free containers. There is still some conservation work to be done.

The first of the approximate 50 feet of papers to be identified, arranged, and described were the manuscripts of the published novels and short story collections. There is at least one stage of each of the books— draft, typescript, galley, or notes—over 200 items, some being as large as the 1146 page manuscript/typescript of For Whom the Bell Tolls; others as small as a page of "Titles" for In Our Time.

After the opening of these papers in January 1975, work progressed to the still-photograph collection and the other 600 or so manuscripts—the short stories, magazine and newspaper articles, poetry, fragmentary and unpublished short pieces—and then to the incoming and outgoing correspondence (more than 1100 Hemingway letters which include original family letters, drafts, carbons, unsent letters, and some copies which were donated or exchanged by individuals and other libraries). As each part of the collection was cataloged, it was copied and opened for research use.

The guide to the collection now exists in card form in the Hemingway Room. Each item or letter is individually identified and carded, and name cross-references and an index are provided. The photographs are also arranged and described, and there is a calendar for the newspaper clipping collection, which includes clippings by, about, sent to, or saved by Hemingway, as well as listings of his journals, books, maps, foreign translations, and personal effects.

As of the dedication, July 18th, 1980, 109 researchers worked with the collection. These have included well-known Hemingway authorities, international scholars, as well as local high-school students. Many of the researchers have visited again and again. Numerous full-length books, dissertations, and journal articles have been researched in the collection. Although certainly only a small number of the people writing on Hemingway have used the collection, it is still interesting to note that there are 136 entries in the 1976 Fitzgerald/Hemingway Annual. In 1977 there are 143; in 1978-171; in 1979-268.

The papers that follow are representative of the wide-range of research, analysis and discussion that awaits those who visit the Hemingway Room. I look forward to welcoming and aiding both returning veteran scholars and student newcomers.

Jo August
Curator, Hemingway Collection
and
Coordinator, "Papers of a Writer"

JFK AND HEMINGWAY

George Plimpton

This is the speech made at a dinner on July 18, 1980, to commemorate the opening of the Hemingway Room in the Kennedy Library on Columbia Point, Boston. In attendance at the dinner—which was held in the great glass-fronted foyer of the I.M. Pei building and at which were served dishes and drinks described in his books (Hemingway's own Papa Doble rum concoction among them)—were members of the Hemingway family (though not Hemingway's widow, Miss Mary, who was indisposed), Mrs. Aristotle Onassis, representing the Library, and more than one hundred Hemingway scholars.

Ladies and gentlemen, Mrs. Onassis, members of the Hemingway family, Hemingway scholars, survivors of Thompson's Island, and the rest of you who have finished this splendid repast. . . . Since we have concluded a meal here, and a number of Papa Dobles (somewhat pinker and weaker than the drink Papa invented, thank goodness), I thought I'd start by telling you of two occasions, both meals, at which I had personal encounters with the two extraordinary men whose names are associated tonight as we celebrate the opening of the Hemingway library room.

First, President Kennedy. Some years ago, I went to a large dinner at the White House, a social evening, and after dinner a few of us were taken on an informal tour of the place by the President, during which at one point, I believe in the Oval office, the President motioned to me and said, "George, I'd like to talk about your grandmother."

I was, as you can imagine, somewhat startled by this request. I should tell you something about my grandmother and why the President wished to talk to me about her. Her father was a civil war "boy" general by the name of Adelbert Ames—winner of two Medals of Honor, the commander of the 20th Maine, wounded at the Battle of Bull Run. He was at Antietam, the Battle of Fredericksburg, at Chancellorsville, and then, in the 11th Corps, at Gettysburg, later at Cold Harbor—just the sort of man that President Kennedy and Ernest Hemingway would have thought the highest of. The trouble was that after the war Adelbert Ames, at the age of 33, became the Governor General, appointed by Abraham Lincoln, of the state of Mississippi, where all you scholars would know he ran afoul of Lucius Quintus Cincinnatus Lamar—the Mississippian who went to Congress and gave the famous eulogy of Charles Sumner, the Radical Republican, which not only earned him a place in the history of reconciliation but also a chapter in President Kennedy's book *Profiles in Courage*. In that chapter Mississippi is described as follows: "No state suffered more from carpetbag rule than Mississippi. Adelbert Ames, first Senator and then Governor, was a native of Maine, a son-in-law of the notorious 'butcher of New Orleans' Benjamin F. Butler. His administration was sustained and nourished by Federal bayonets." On and on.

Well, my grandmother, when she ran across this affront not only to her father but her grandfather, began writing letters to the then-Senator Kennedy explaining that he had really got it all wrong, at least about Adelbert Ames (she was willing to forgo Ben Butler), that he had fallen into the trap of believing those historians who had given the Reconstruction a bad name across the board, and that there were obviously men of integrity and distinction and honor who had served in the South, that Adelbert Ames was one of these men of integrity, and that she wished that Mr. Kennedy would change these offending chapters about her father and get it correct. She wrote quite a lot of these letters. Senator Kennedy wrote her back, of course, saying that it was true—there was a revisionist swing in consideration of the Reconstruction and it was likely that there was a lot to say for her views but that he was stuck with his position and that was that. Besides, he went on to say, it was very unlikely that there would be subsequent editions of *Profiles in Courage*. The deed had been done, right or wrong.

Then, of course, the Senator went on to become the President of the United States and there were a number of subsequent editions of *Profiles in Courage,* and in a lot of languages too—each of which went on about Ames' administration in Mississippi being "nourished by Federal bayonets" and these induced, of course, further letters to the White House on the part of my grandmother.

It was this that the President wished to speak to me about.

He enlisted my aid, asked me if there were any way this steady flow of letters could be stopped. Could I persuade my grandmother to cease and desist? It was cutting into the work of the government.

I said the only way was to change *Profiles in Courage*—that, after all, my grandmother was a Massachusetts woman, and as the President well knew that species was especially resilient and uncompromising.

I didn't actually say that, but I wanted to. What I said, of course, was that I quite understood the President's position and I would see what I could do.

Then the President did the most remarkable thing. He asked me, "How much do you know about your great grandfather—Adelbert Ames?"

Well, I said that I knew some of the family stories about him, that as a boy of seven or eight I actually remembered him, looking into the eyes of this elderly man—he died at 98—sitting in a rocking-chair with a shawl over his knees and realizing even then that I was looking into the eyes that had seen Pickett's charge at Gettysburg. And the President said, "Well, do you know what your great grandfather's favorite epithet was?" I looked surprised and said no. The President said, "Well, when your great grandfather commanded the 20th Maine he was famous for reviewing his troops and if he saw anyone slouching, or whose posture was atrocious, he would stand in front of this miscreant and shout out at the top of his lungs, 'For God's sake, draw up your bowels!' " The President gave this quite a "reading," as they say in the theatrical business. He drew himself up and he delivered this line very much as Adelbert Ames must have delivered it out on those New England parade grounds a century before. It caused no end of quick consternation in the Oval Office. The two or three people in there looked around with startled looks and I suppose they wondered, My God, what's Plimpton done now? The doors flew open and the sergeants-at-arms rushed in. But I think I must have been the most startled person there—to think that a President of the United States knew more about my great grandfather, a relatively obscure Civil War hero, than I did. . . . And I remember observing to myself how fortunate it was that the country was being served by an intellect to which such astonishingly obscure details could be drawn to mind with such ease. As a matter of fact, I ran across verification of what President Kennedy had shouted at me subsequently in John J. Pullen's book, *The 20th Maine*—there's the line tucked away in that book just as President Kennedy delivered it.

You may want to know what my grandmother went on to do. When it was apparent that *Profiles in Courage* was not going to be dismantled and put together again to suit her views, she did what any sensible Massachusetts woman would do: she sat down and wrote her own book . . . a biography of her father entitled *Integrity,* printed by the University of Columbia Press. It's much longer than *Profiles in Courage*—nearly 700 pages. Lucius Lamar doesn't come off all that well in it. She is very polite and understanding about the President. It weighs four or five pounds. She worked on it for eight years and was blind and in her eighties when she finished it. President Kennedy surely would have applauded her determination and the fact that *Integrity* (I went and looked in the files and discovered that the book is not here) is arriving post-haste next week. He would know that a Massachusetts woman will eventually have her way . . . even if it's through the agency of her grandson and thus *Integrity* will proudly supplement the packing cases of those letters of hers that doubtless are somewhere (breathing slightly I have the feeling) in this building.

Now, the meal with Hemingway. In 1958 I was privileged enough to be allowed to conduct an interview on the "craft of writing" with him for the literary magazine, then in its fifth year, the *Paris Review*. I think he agreed to appear in the magazine despite its terribly limited circulation, because he, of course, was first published in magazines very much like the *Paris Review*—the *Double Dealer*, in which both he and William Faulkner in one issue appeared for the first time in print; *Transition*; the *Transatlantic Review*; Ezra Pound's *Exile*. But he didn't enjoy talking about writing. He felt it was a sort of draining operation, like drawing water from a well that wasn't replenished that easily. So whenever I asked him a question it was always with a faint wince that perhaps the response would be physical instead of verbal. One morning we were coming back from fishing in the Gulf Stream—coming into the little harbor at Cohima, Cuba, and it had been just the best day out there. . . . Papa in his element, at his very best, amusing and informative, and we might have had a true Papa Doble or two, and he had showed me how you look for the big fish where the man o'war birds duck down to the ocean, because it meant the bait fish were there, and the big fish underneath, driving them up, and I hadn't gotten seasick, and he seemed in the best of his moods when we stepped up onto the dock from the boat. I thought it was as good a time as any to ask him something which had always puzzled me because it was so unlike anything else in his writing—namely the use of the image of the bird when he writes about sex. There are a number of examples—in the Indian stories; and perhaps the most striking example, the white bird that flies out of the gondola when Colonel Cantwell and the Italian Princess are making love in there in *Across the River and Into the Trees*. I'm not sure that any novelist is comfortable writing about love-making —they so often seem all thumbs at it—to put it awkwardly myself—and certainly Hemingway isn't easy with it. I mean "the earth moves" and all that business, and so perhaps this touched some sensitive chord. Because when I asked, "Papa, what is the significance of the white bird that sometimes turns up in your, ah, sex scenes?"—well, my goodness, it was as if I had jabbed him with a fork. He wheeled around, his whiskers bristling like an alarmed cat's and he asked me this extraordinary question, considering it came from a Nobel Prize winning author and was addressed to someone whose only book published to date was a children's book entitled *The Rabbit's Umbrella*. "Well, I suppose you think," the great man said, "you can do any better?"

Well, I said, "No, no, Papa, certainly not."

He carried this anger up to lunch at the Finca. Three of us were there, Papa, Miss Mary, and myself, really four because Hemingway had this cat that sat next to his plate, Christobal—a sort of Roman emperor of a cat, who lay there, absolutely supine, and from time to time it would drop its head back, and Hemingway would drop a morsel of food down its throat. Well, Hemingway and his wife got into an argument—a sort of Mr. and Mrs. argument except it was about how many lions they had seen around a water-hole on safari the year before. Hemingway said that they had seen eight lions, and Miss Mary said eleven, something like that, and she said she could prove it was eleven because she'd written it up in her diary, and he said that didn't prove anything because it took an experienced eye to count lions milling around a water-hole, and their voices were rising, when all of a sudden Hemingway looked across the table at me, and it was as if he were looking at me for the first time.

At that time, I should explain, I had not long before, in the interests of my odd career as a participatory journalist fought—if that's the proper word—the lightheavyweight champion of the world, a man by the name of Archie Moore, the Mongoose they used to call him, and there was one appalling statistic that he had in the record books—namely, that he had knocked out more people than anyone else in the history of the ring. As this fight had approached, Hemingway had become very interested in it. He kept asking me to come out to Ketchum, Idaho, to go through some serious training. I had the sense that he thought I was truly going after Mr. Moore's title. He wrote me a little letter about what to do about the left hook. I can't quite remember what that was . . . it was either to do one thing or the other, and I'm not going to guess and tell you because the letter was stolen and I might give you the wrong information. He kept urging me to fight a few tune-up bouts. "The elephant hunter," he once told me, "can't begin to call himself an elephant hunter until his fiftieth elephant."

All of this I slipped and dodged like a very classy lightweight. As you can see, I am not properly equipped to fight anyone. I have a very thin, delicate nose, which bleeds at the slightest touch. Not only that, but I suffer from a phenomenon known as "sympathetic response," which means that I weep at the slightest touch. I only barely managed to survive the fight with Moore, mostly I think at his bewilderment at being in the ring with a man both bleeding and weeping. He held me up for three rounds. I didn't especially want to be held up. I wanted to go down. He kept whispering in my ear, "Breathe, man breathe."

Hemingway was fascinated by all this. And suddenly at this luncheon, full of rage because of the little inconsequential argument he was having with his wife about the number of lions they had seen at some obscure African water-hole, he looked across at me—I had the sense of a gazelle being stared at by a lion across a tuft of grass—and he said: "Let's see how good you are."

I had no idea what he was talking about at first, but then as he came around the dining-room table I could see that he was in a semi-crouch, his hands bunched at his waist, and I realized he wanted to *fight*. So I pushed back my chair and stood up with this enormous smile on my face, as if this were all going to be good fun. I stuck out a long tentative jab and no sooner had I done so, when bang, the left hook that Hemingway had sent me that letter about, and which I hadn't studied sufficiently, came up from the vicinity of his belt and he whacked me alongside the face. No bleeding, thank goodness, but quite a lot of sympathetic response.

What was I to do? I couldn't imagine myself leaping out the window and hot-footing it to the distant city of Havana. Christobal, still lolling on the table, was absolutely no help; neither was Miss Mary, her head down as she picked at her salad.

I then suddenly had a stroke of inspiration. I dropped my hands and asked him a question—"How did you do that? How did you bring your hands up from that position?"—turning him into an instructor, asking him in such wonder about this left hook that he was enormously flattered. A smile appeared through those white whiskers.

"Counterpunch," he announced.

He was as pleased as an inventor showing off a machine. He showed me what he had done. I was cuffed around a bit more, but it was to illustrate a point, not as a target of his frustration.

Miss Mary looked up from her salad and smiled at us. I remember hoping she wasn't going to butt into the nice time we were having and insist on the number of lions she'd seen on that Africa day long past. . . .

President Kennedy and Ernest Hemingway never had a meal together. . . . I'm not sure I would have wanted to be there if they had. Time spent with one, singly, was quite enough. Heaven knows what having lunch with the pair of them would have done to my sense of well-being. . . .

Since there are so many scholars here, I suppose it would be of interest to them as to why these papers, this Hemingway Collection, is here, not in Oak Park, or Ketchum, or Key West, or the Ritz Bar in Paris, or next to Harry's Bar in Venice, or perhaps the Plaza Mayor in Pamplona, or Nairobi, or some place, in short, with which one identifies the name of Hemingway. Boston, for all its intellectual values, its men of letters, is not exactly an area synonymous with the Hemingway legend. It has a Ritz, but it is not Hemingway's Ritz. It has a fish, the cod, but that is not Hemingway's fish. I once asked Miss Mary if it were not because Hemingway had always professed a liking for Harvard. He had once told me that if he had ever gone to college—which, of course, he didn't—he would have picked Harvard. "Why Harvard?" I asked Miss Mary. "I haven't the faintest notion," she replied—and she said it as if that were the obvious answer to the question of why *anyone* should want to go there.

Well, here is the true story. A couple of months after Hemingway died, Miss Mary called Bill Walton, an artist and old-time friend who had known her and Ernest when all three were correspondents in Europe during World War II. And she asked Walton if there were any way Pres-

ident Kennedy could help her get to Cuba (of course relations had col-
lapsed completely then) in order to get out of the Finca Vigia, outside
Havana, all his papers, and paintings, and the memorabilia that had been
left behind after the Revolution in 1960. Bill Walton went to see the
President, who was enormously sympathetic to Miss Mary's problems,
and was able to set the machinery in motion to get her in there in spite of
the travel-ban and other barriers that perhaps would have made it more
provident and less awkward for him to say, well, that's something we
can't do at this time.

Miss Mary went. She went to see Mr. Castro himself, whom she found,
in her words, "pleasant and agreeable and" (only someone with Miss
Mary's spunkiness would have the conviction to say this) "better informed about politics than I expected."

In any case, Miss Mary gave the Finca and its library not to him, but to
the Cuban nation, and in return was permitted to remove the paintings and
drawings, a few of the more valuable books, and Papa's papers—all of
which—with the exception of the famous Miró painting which Papa
bought in Paris for 350 francs and is now insured for a quarter of a million
dollars and which will go to the National Gallery in Washington—are here
in this building.

The reason the collection is here is that Miss Mary had always been
very grateful for President Kennedy's seeing to it that she could get to
Cuba and back, and when she asked Bill Walton what she could do to
show her appreciation, that was his recommendation, that the best way to
say thank you would be to leave the papers to the library which bears the
name of the man who had been so helpful to her.

I know that Mrs. Onassis—because she told me about it—would want it
said how much she, and all of us, indeed, should express homage to Miss
Mary for her steadfastness once she decided to give her husband's papers
to the Library—rather like trying to get a suitcase on a balky camel
considering the odyssey of the Library from the car barns of Cambridge to
its variety of prospective sites—and yet never during those fifteen years
did Miss Mary ever feel that this Library, however peripatetic, wasn't the
place she wanted her husband's papers to rest.

Now that they are here on Columbia Point she must be enormously
pleased—this magic site of seawater and air, its entrance to the sea beyond, all of it so appropriate.

Of course, there are similarities to be made—Kennedy and Hemingway. They both set styles in their comparative fields which will be remembered for their distinctiveness—the Hemingway style, the Kennedy
years—phrases which connote a certain advocacy of skill, purity of expression, form, a horror of injustice, a focus on performance. They both
admired people of conviction. Hemingway once tried a generalization—

which he hated doing—and said that a writer without a sense of justice and injustice would be better off editing the Year Book of a school for exceptional children than writing novels. He said that the most essential gift for a good writer was a built-in, shock-proof detector of cant and nonsense and injustice—that's not *quite* the way he put it but it will do for this company—it was a writer's radar, he went on to say, and all great writers had it . . . as do the best of our leaders. . . .

It is ironic, in a sense, that President Kennedy and Ernest Hemingway never met. They came close once—when Kennedy (he was the Massachusetts senator then) went to Cuba to visit his friend, Ambassador Earl E.T. Smith. Phone calls were made. Papa hoped that the young senator would come out to the Finca for lunch, but, alas, there were conflicts and the luncheon and the meeting of these two remarkable men never took place. One imagines they would have had a fine time. Kennedy would have made Hemingway feel better about politicians, possibly, and Hemingway would have made Kennedy feel easier about novelists.

If Hemingway's health had been better, the two could have met at the Inaugural in 1960. Hemingway was invited. He was in the Mayo Clinic in Rochester, Minnesota, at the time, and it was an especially bad time for him because the doctors had told him that he was not well enough to leave—a realization, really for the first time, of seeing himself behind bars . . . and it was at this time that the President's personal invitation arrived. It moved him enormously. It was a marvelous and lifting moment for him, according to those who were there, though in fact the doctors would not change their minds and let him go to Washington. What a vision that would have been for us to remember—Ernest Hemingway in the stands on that frozen extraordinary day!

Hemingway did watch the ceremony on television and afterwards he sent a communication to the President:

> Watching the Inauguration from Rochester there was the happiness and the hope and the pride and how beautiful we thought Mrs. Kennedy was and how deeply moving the inaugural address. Watching on the screen I was sure our President would stand any of the heat to come as he had taken the cold of that day. Each day since, I have renewed my faith and tried to understand the practical difficulties of governing he must face as they arise and admire the true courage he brings to them. It is a good thing to have a brave man as our President in times as tough as these are for our country and the world.

Sheridan wrote somewhat mockingly in *The Critic* that "Conscience has no more to do with gallantry than it has to do with politics"—a sentiment that both Hemingway and Kennedy took issue with in their careers. "The world is a fine place and worth fighting for," is the important phrase out of *For Whom the Bell Tolls*. It is echoed in that message Hemingway sent President Kennedy after the Inauguration: "It is a good thing to have a brave man as our president in times as tough as these are for our country and the world."

So, how appropriate this union! Robert Frost was always talking about feats of association. Putting this and that together. That connective click! He was talking about the performance of the poet, but he could well have been talking about the fortuity of this particular association that we are gathered here to celebrate tonight . . . art and government in the name of the best of both, housed together so expeditiously on this lovely Massachusetts shore.

UNEXPLORED TERRITORY: THE NEXT TEN YEARS OF HEMINGWAY STUDIES*

Michael S. Reynolds

We meet today on an island—not in the stream exactly, but what has become the mainstream of Hemingway studies. Those who were at the Alabama Hemingway Conference in 1976 will remember Jackson Benson exhorting people to get down into the trenches to begin the difficult scholarship required. At Alabama, the camp was divided. Some were still repeating the type of criticism that others felt had been at least temporarily exhausted. At that conference, I urged everyone to come to the Kennedy Library, for the manuscripts could not be ignored. It was here that our critical inheritance would be tested, proved and revised. For the Hemingway scholar, the PMLA bibliography is no longer sufficient. Carlos Baker and Philip Young remain our guides over Hemingway terrain, but there is much unexplored territory yet to be mapped.

That exploration, that future is an act of the imagination. It will happen, of course, for someone is always ready to invent it. I want to share with you an imaginary future in Hemingway studies. I would not be so presumptuous as to insist that it is the only possible future. Call it, rather, a position paper—a basis others might use, modify, or reject in making their own maps. If I had time enough and intensity, this is the work I would do.

The heart of the matter is housed, obviously, in the Kennedy Library. The manuscript collection with its drafts, typescripts, fragments, letters and pictures is the territory itself. Averaging two weeks a year for the last six years in the manuscripts, I still have only the roughest outline of the collection. To map it thoroughly, every resource must be used. Gradually over the last decade a number of important tools have been made available. At Yale's Beinecke Library, the Gertrude Stein and Ezra Pound papers are open. There, also, are Charles Fenton's papers—interviews with sources now dead, interviews only partially exploited. At the University of Texas, the correspondence of Hemingway's parents is open. At the University of Virginia, along with the Dos Passos papers, is a rich Hemingway collection, including the holograph manuscript of *The Green Hills of Africa*. Robert O. Stephens, whose study of the non-fiction is superb, has recently collected the critical reception for us. We have Matthew Bruccoli's numerous publications in which important primary material is preserved. In October, Princeton University Press will publish my inventory of Hemingway's reading between 1910 and 1940. The parallel volume which will include the Cu-

*Portions of this article are adapted from *Hemingway's Reading 1910-1940* (to be published by Princeton Univ. Press, 1980).

ban years will be soon finished by Professors Brasch and Sigman. This fall we will have 800 pages of Hemingway letters, edited by Carlos Baker. We also have Baker's biography—the names, the places and how the weather was. We have Mary's autobiography. Audre Hanneman has given us one of the sharpest tools of all—her wonderful two-volume bibliography. We are rich in basic tools. How best to use them is the question. Let me count the ways that I would go.

First, and perhaps most difficult, is the matter of texts. This Christmas in Houston, Paul Smith will moderate an MLA panel on this very topic. To whet your appetites for those papers, let me gloss the problem. Quite simply, we do not have definitive texts. Anyone who has worked with the drafts, typescripts and galleys of a single Hemingway book knows there are errors and omissions. We would be surprised if there were not. The climate is not yet right for the standard editions to be done, but in the next ten years, the work will begin. In the interim, there are other texts which we do not have at all. We still do not have the complete edition of Hemingway's journalism, either early or late. To read his piece "A Veteran Visits Old Front" from 1922, we still must order microfilm from the Toronto *Star*. On the basis of letters and fragments here at the Kennedy, I think there are still unidentified Hemingway articles in the *Star*. Other loose ends need knitting up. Pursuing clues in the Stein collection, I'm on the track of Hemingway's review of Stein's *Geography and Plays*, for example. Discovered, it will not measurably change anyone's views, but written and published, it must be added to the corpus. Another useful text would be the collection of all Hemingway interviews and public statements on his art. The one other obvious book we need is the bibliography of the collection itself, which I have urged Jo August to publish. Once that bibliography is done, the problems and possibilities, which I am outlining, will be obvious to everyone.

Those of us interested in editing the texts should begin with textual study itself. As Professor Oldsey and I will assure you, all it takes is time, patience and more time. Right now we have all the materials open to do a fine study of *For Whom the Bell Tolls*. I am not about to do this "Hemingway's Second War," but someone should. While working in the manuscripts, we should help each other by suggesting dates for the numerous fragments and unpublished material.

Before the really deep digging can begin, we must first complete the basic research. What remains is neither glamorous nor easy, but it is necessary. For example, at Stanford University, housed in largely uncataloged crates are the WWI field records of the American Red Cross. Hemingway and Dos Passos material is there. Someone else needs to dig through the U. S. Army archives on data on Hemingway's World War II experience in Europe. This may be zero research; conversely, it may illuminate *Across the River and Into the Trees*. Would it be worth the dusty search? I don't know. But I do know that public records are more trustworthy on particular points than is memory long after the event. Newspapers, for example, have still to be examined. The Paris edition of the *Herald Tribune*, almost impossible to locate on microfilm, is a treasure trove of the Twenties. More tedious to read, the Key West newspaper during the Thirties cannot be ignored for a thorough job on Hemingway's years there. No one has gone through the Key West county records, court records, police records.

The only way to approach such research is free of all theses. To paraphrase Brecht: data first, then ideas. Without a thesis to prove, one cannot be selective. Bring back all the data. Later, when you've made use of it, give it to the Kennedy so that all of us might share. I have just donated all of my files on Hemingway's Milan nurse, Agnes Von Kurowsky. I have no further use for the material, but, needless to say, my version of it has been biased. The complete transcript of her interview, her Red Cross files, and her pictures will be here for others to slant. In the near future, I will send a copy of Hemingway's FBI file, which Rod Cockshutt, a colleague of mine at NCSU, has broken loose under the freedom of information act. It contains 107 sanitized pages with 17 more pages deleted. Begun in the early Forties, the file tells us more, perhaps, about the FBI than about Hemingway, but it does provide a basis for his paranoia described by Mary in *How It Was*.

To this point, I suspect that future exploration does not sound terribly exciting. Perhaps not. The gold rush, you see, is over. Nothing is left on the surface for the picking. The old territory has been so well mapped that only tourists are going there this season. The old veins are exhausted. To open new mines requires deep digging and heavy equipment at costs that were once unfeasible. During the next ten years, our most important piece of heavy equipment will be the computer. In compiling and analyzing Hemingway's reading, 1910-to-1940, I discovered that one need not be a computer expert to use the computer, any more than one needs to be an expert mechanic to drive a car. Any decent university computer center can provide a programmer. Once the program is functioning smoothly, a child can run it.

First we need data bases. We need to put the entire existing text of Hemingway's fiction on to computer tape and cards. This project requires no imagination: the programs are readily available. It will take money to pay keypunch operators, but once it is done, the data base will be marketable. More difficult and more time consuming will be putting the Hanneman critical bibliography into the computer. As useful as that bibliography already is, the sheer size of it is formidable. Titles do not always indicate subject matter. If it were entered with a detailed subject code, article by article, book by book, then a computer search would give us an instantaneous printout on a particular subject: Africa, for example. Anyone who has been to the Library of Congress lately knows that computer search by subject matter is already a reality. As we sit here today, most major libraries are converting all their card catalogues to the computer. At NCSU, I have a tape of Hemingway's earlier reading that is entered by subject, title, author, genre, year, and source, copies of which I hope eventually to make available at cost.

Once we have the data bases, objective analysis will supplement what has heretofore been mostly subjective. At its simplest level, the computer does four functions well: it counts quickly; it has instantaneous recall; it makes comparisons; and it measures change over time. Some obvious possibilities include: comparative studies of word usage, syntax, and style; style changes over time; and content analysis. At a more complex level, the textual data base will allow us one day to edit on the computer. As far as I know, such a program is not yet written, but then I don't know much about computers. Having watched a colleague of mine spend five years editing a single text by Cooper, his desk buried under tiny file boxes of yellowing note cards, I vowed I would never get into the editing business. But once I saw a mere fraction of the computer's potential, I realized that future editors would be working from interactive terminals.

As a final example of computer-aided research, let me return to my own program at NCSU. From a few simple commands, all of them in recognizable English, the computer will tell me what poetry Hemingway read in 1925; what African books he read in 1932-33; all of the books he read on the Spanish Civil War. It will give me all of the poetry he read between 1910 and 1940, arranging it year by year and inside each year by either author or title. The results are more significant than you might expect. Before writing *The Green Hills of Africa*, Hemingway read every book he could find on African exploration, including numerous books long out of print. Thirty years of his poetry reading prints out at 136 entries. Not bad for a kid who never went to college.

For those of us interested in literary history and literary biography, there are farther fields yet to develop. Now that Mary Hemingway has judiciously lifted the restrictions on the letters, the author's literary relationships can be explored as never before. One obvious book for the next decade will be called "The Hemingway-Perkins Correspondence." I don't mean simply printing both sides of the correspondence in chronological order, although that is part of it. The book I want to read will illuminate the professional lives of the writer and the editor with the light of their times: the social, historical, political, as well as literary light. The meticulous filing habits of Perkins have made this job easier than it might have been. Between the Kennedy collection of Perkins' letters and the Princeton collection of Hemingway letters and Perkins' carbons, the data are available. The hard part will be placing them into their milieu.

Ideally, the work would be a collaboration between Scott Berg, our Perkins expert, and someone who knows the Hemingway side with equal authority. I know that we have no history for such collaboration, but we must learn from the social and the pure scientists. Future work, to be authoritative, demands cooperation. None of us has either the time or training to master all the material alone. For example, Professor Oldsey and I, literally simultaneously, have both done studies of *A Farewell to Arms*. Between the two of us, we've done two decent books. Had we been collaborating, I think we could have done a single, fine book, probably better than the sum of the two.

What I am suggesting, if not joint authorship, is at least cooperation, both inter and intramural. Carlos Baker, with his boundless generosity, has set the tone for such cooperation. More than a few of us, myself included, have benefitted from his storehouse of data and experience. To use the Hemingway letters for literary history, we must cooperate. How else can we do what needs to be done: for example, the literary relationships between Hemingway and Pound, Fitzgerald, Thornton Wilder, Dos Passos, and Stein. These all remain only partially explored; now that we can bring their literary lives together, as Forrest Read did for Pound and Joyce, a clearer history of the Twenties will appear, a period seemingly exhausted. I think the difficult work there is just beginning.

My next suggestion is perhaps the most obvious one: the literary biography of Ernest Hemingway. For the last ten years, every project I have worked on has also been done simultaneously by someone else; therefore, I feel certain that any number of persons are already at work on the literary biography. In *Ernest Hemingway: A Life Story*, Baker tells us in the preface that he is not writing "what is commonly called a 'critical biography,'" in which the biographer seeks to explore, analyze, and evaluate the full range of his subject's literary output simultaneously with the record of his life" (p. x). Baker adds that his biography is not definitive, that "many lines of investigation remain to be followed out" (p. x). One such line of investigation is the literary biography: the artistic development of Hemingway, the writer, in the political and intellectual milieu of his time. Such a study breaks into four periods: the first stage begins with the early years in Oak Park, ending in Paris in 1921; the following stages are the Paris years through 1929; the Key West years to 1940; and finally the post-Forty years. Four years ago the material was available to begin the Oak Park and Paris years—all the data except his reading, which I saw was crucial. While researching the first two periods, I began culling the reading from various sources. With that tool now finely honed, I hope, within three years, to have Hemingway's literary biography between 1910-1929 finished. From memoirs, interviews, public records, newspapers, reading lists, manuscripts, letters, books, and the Baker biography, I think I can assemble a plausible fiction. All biography is, of course, fiction.

Already I have spent a good deal of time in Oak Park, not the most exciting place in the Midwest. I will probably do more time there. The most valuable lesson I've learned so far is trust no one, not other writers, not even yourself, especially not yourself. Doubt every assumption until it proves true. Otherwise you will step over rocks that have never been looked under. In researching my first book, I discovered that although every Hemingway scholar had written the Red Cross Archives in Washington, none had actually gone there. Because I made the effort to go not once but three times, eventually I got access to Agnes Von Kurowsky's complete file. In Oak Park, everyone has made his obligatory pilgrimage to the local high school; there, proud administrators display the Hemingway material, now locked in the vault. But no one had ever asked about the courses or the required reading from those early years. I was told that the records had disappeared. Finally I had the good sense to ask a secretary what she did with dead files. She said she would probably store them in the attic of the old building. In that dusty attic on a hot June day, I found exactly what I was looking for. Paper has a way of outlasting people, outlasting trees. My basic assumption, always, is that nothing is ever lost, only misfiled.

In attempting the literary biography of Hemingway's early years, I am not choosing the richest field, for, as we all know, that period has already been severely prospected. The choice was one of necessity: I had too much research time invested not to write about it. The truly unexplored territory is the Key West period, which, during the next decade, will probably be the most rewarding field. If I were starting from scratch today, that's where I would work. The Thirties were by far Hemingway's most productive period, and his most stable. He wrote essays, journalism, one movie, one play, non-fiction, short stories, and novels. The range of style and genre is greater than any period before or after. Yet, we always give it short shrift. It is as if he were dormant between *A Farewell to Arms* and *For Whom the Bell Tolls*. The non-fiction—*Death in the Afternoon* and *The Green Hills of Africa*—has been largely ignored; maybe the New Critics couldn't deal with non-fiction. As a result I suspect we have badly misread Hemingway's experiments. If a writer is attempting to play the man-of-letters role, then we must judge his entire performance, not just the fiction. Therefore, do not believe what you have read about his Thirties work. Do not believe that *To Have and Have Not* is as bad as some have said. Above all else, do not believe Hemingway's foreward to *The Green Hills of Africa*, which tells us:

> Unlike many novels, none of the characters or incidents in this book is imaginary. . . . The writer has attempted to write an absolutely true book to see whether the shape of a country and the pattern of a month's action can, if truly presented, compete with a work of the imagination.

If you believe this statement to be the entire import of the book, you should never buy life insurance, stocks, or cars of any sort. If ever an author gave us a book on his aesthetics, *Green Hills* is such a book. One reading of the manuscript will show the careful craftsmanship. The most cursory comparison with *Death in the Afternoon* will show the difference in intent. Let me repeat: although we call these books non-fiction, there is no non-fiction. All writing is fiction, in a sense.

I do not think it is too soon for us to begin a serious treatment of Hemingway's various fictions in the Thirties. God knows they have been massively ignored. Turn again to the Hanneman bibliography. Up to 1975, we wrote more critical commentary on "The Short Happy Life of Francis Macomber" than we did on *Death in the Afternoon, The Green Hills of Africa*, and *To Have and Have Not* combined. On *A Farewell to Arms,* there have been over one hundred critical books and articles. On *Death in the Afternoon*, only five. Here is the truly uncharted territory: barely fingered manuscripts and virgin public records. I beg several of you to stake your claims, to begin the hard, necessary work here. If you would make the trek into this territory that I have sketched out, I advise you to read Auden's sequence, *The Quest*. Particularly you might memorize:

> Suppose he's listened to the erudite committee,
> He would have only found where not to look.

Nothing I have suggested so far is either easy or quick. All of these projects will take years, not months. A week working in the Kennedy manuscripts is only a beginning; a month, but a fair start. If anyone needs immediate returns, I advise investment in a different author. The further terrain I am about to suggest is in some ways even more precarious than what has preceded. Many of the suggestions are based on patterns I have seen in Hemingway's reading. Many are speculative. For a complete version of my analysis, scholars will have to wait until the book appears this fall. To whet the collective appetite and perhaps increase the sale, let me preview some of the patterns and their implications. My proofs are too detailed to belabor here, but they are part of the book.

Early in the Twenties, Hemingway jotted himself a significant note, which he preserved for us:

> Education consists in finding sources obscure enough to
> imitate so that they will be perfectly safe. (Item 489)

If that sounds like a young man's gloss of Eliot and Pound, we shouldn't be surprised. Hemingway owned almost everything those two masters wrote, and he read the early material on Pound's knee. For too many years, we have made false assumptions about what Hemingway must have read. The writer himself has misled us with his public statements about his reading.

He read the books on the lists he gave us; he just didn't give us a complete list. In another unpublished fragment, he tells us:

> It is not un-natural that the best writers are liars. A major part of their trade
> is to lie or invent and they will lie when they are drunk, or to themselves, or to

strangers. They often lie unconsciously and then remember their lies with deep remorse. If they knew all other writers were liars too it would cheer them up. (Item 845)

Then, too, we have lied to ourselves. The insistence, in our time, on a unique and self-contained American literature has worked against our best interests. In graduate school we may treat it as separate from British literature, but, American authors born before WWI had only the sketchiest notion of an American tradition. More often, and particularly in Hemingway's case, they were grounded in the British tradition. As a result, many of us know too little about the cultural roots of our man. For example, in 1940 when Hemingway packed his working library for his move to Cuba, he took 800 books. Eighty-eight percent of them were either by British or Continental authors. Of the American authors, almost all were his contemporaries. No matter which way you slice the twenty-three hundred books in my inventory of his reading, the same pattern appears: 25% American; 25% continental; 50% British. At least half of the British and continental writers are not his contemporaries.

During his formative years, few, if any, of Hemingway's models of excellence were American. Later he might say that it all started with *Huck Finn*, but when he began his own picaresque novel (still unpublished), he thought of it in terms of *Tom Jones*. *Torrents of Spring* he compared with *Joseph Andrews* and *Shamela*.[1] He sounds American, but his roots are British. His earliest concepts of subject matter, structure and style were influenced by neither the American realists nor the naturalists. The American writers of the 1890s were largely a deferred generation for him. He had to go to Paris to discover Stephen Crane. Twain and James were his only significant contact with the American tradition, and he did not savor James until he met Ezra Pound.

From 1921 until he died, Hemingway bought or borrowed 150-200 books a year. Now someone is sure to say that having a book is no assurance that he read it. No such claims are being made. He may have read none of them. Unlikely, but possible. For those critics who prefer the "dumb-ox" version of Hemingway, no evidence is likely to change their minds. The rest of us will have to deal with his reading patterns as our lights guide us. Some of these patterns suggest radically different approaches to the Hemingway territory, approaches which will be surveyed during the next ten years.

Computer-counting the entire inventory by genre shows that after fiction the genre that appears most frequently is biography: 297 entries, many of them literary biographies. The three lives he was early most interested in were D. H. Lawrence, T. E. Lawrence of the Arabs, and Lord Byron. Romantics all, these men had led monumental public lives, which, as Hemingway should have noted, eventually dwarfed their writing. Foreign travel, sexual extravagance, beards, costumes, adopted countries, bizarre behavior, heroism, isolation, the grand gesture—it wasn't their literature but their lives Hemingway absorbed. Of course, their lives do come out in his writing as well. Think of Robert Jordan—and then think of Lawrence among his Arabs. Byron had his Greece, Hemingway his Spain. Long ago Carlos Baker suggested that Hemingway was a neo-romantic. I, for one, had resisted this view as long as possible. In the reading's light, I must confess myself now a true believer. Moral behavior in Hemingway, partially at least, is rooted in the lives of the two Lawrences and Byron.

What I am talking about, of course, is that illusive topic—the "code" by which the Hemingway protagonist sustains himself. For too long we have been looking in the wrong directions. A code figure appears frequently in the early reading. The lives of General Marbot and General Grant contain part of it. The lives of T. E. Lawrence and Byron contain other parts. But the archtype has been obvious all along: another warrior, little connected with Hemingway, whose presence has been obscured by our own critical blinders—the medieval knight. As usual, Carlos Baker called our attention to Col. Cantwell's "chivalric code,"[2] but no one followed Baker's lead. Hemingway's high school reading and his reading in Paris during the Twenties show a continued interest in the knight figure. Immediately after writing *A Farewell to Arms*, Hemingway read several books on the medieval period. In 1934, Scott Fitzgerald wrote Max Perkins a curious letter, seeking information about Hemingway's work in progress:

> Needless to say I am highly curious about the setting of his [Hemingway's] novel. I hope to God it is not the crusading story he once had in mind, for I would hate like hell for my 9th century novel to compete with *that*.[3]

The last time the two authors had been in close contact was the spring and summer of 1929. Hemingway never wrote the novel Fitzgerald feared; Fitzgerald never completed his own. But those chapters he did publish have a knight figure for whom Hemingway seems to be the prototype.

After *A Farewell to Arms*, Hemingway's fiction began to change. His characters in the Twenties—Jake Barnes, Nick Adams, Frederick Henry—do little heroic but survive. It is in the Thirties, just after his last spate of medieval reading, that his characters begin behaving like heros. Harry Morgan, Robert Jordan, and Col. Cantwell, who love truly, end up heroically dead. I suggest that Col. Cantwell and Chaucer's Knight are of closer kin than is readily apparent, that the narrator of *Green Hills of Africa*, pursuing beauty, is on a knight's quest. The scholar who follows this open-ended suggestion will have to repack his safari kit. The old list of necessaries no longer applies. In fact, a Medievalist would have an easier time of it than someone trained exclusively in American literature.

The unexplored territory is full of unwritten books and articles. We still do not have the final word on Hemingway's relationship with Spain. In his reading, we see it wasn't just the bull ring that interested him, although that was the focus. The Spanish study requires a linguist, one who knows the traditions and the literature. With three major books, one play, one movie and several short stories set in Spain, Hemingway left us a challenge still only partially answered.

Could he really read Spanish that well? Once you have seen his reading, there will be no question about his linguistic skills. During the Thirties, he and Pauline read all of Simenon in French. When he packed his books for Cuba, twenty percent of them were in a foreign language. A man does not carry dead weight on such a trip. Evidence says he read Spanish and French fluently, Italian passably, German a little. The twenty-five crates of Cuban-bound books included those writers upon whom he had come to rely, just as a hunter favors particular cartridges with particular loads. He took some writers for reference, some for style, others as classics. His book crates outnumbered all other possessions. Not planning to return, he could not take unnecessary chances. Some writers, he knew, were "born only to help another writer to write one sentence" (*Green Hills*, p. 21). Books were his craft, his art, his metier. Books, he once told Chink Dorman-Smith, were his ammunition. If we want to understand his kills, then we must begin by studying his weaponry and his ammunition. The reading inventory is the first step to such a study.

In the inventory, another obvious and necessary study is Hemingway and Africa. As with Spain, his fascination and his study go beyond the obvious. Begun in Oak Park, his African interest never ended. In high school, he promised himself that he would one day become an explorer; Africa was one of his dreams. Still unpublished is his last journey to that continent in the Fifties. We cannot finish the African study until Mary publishes that work, but we can begin. My own predilection is to begin with maps, whose importance to Hemingway I have demonstrated in *Hemingway's First War*. Part of the Kennedy collection is maps owned by Hemingway. Maps, as Hayakawa told us, are not the territory itself, but they are the starting point. The smaller the scale, the greater the detail. There is a wealth of fine detail in Hemingway's African writing. There is a greater wealth of African reading beneath the surface of that writing.

Other literary relationships in the inventory are less extensive, but no less difficult. Twain, as Philip Young demonstrated and Hemingway affirmed, was important. Huck Finn is there early in the work. But when he packed those Cuban crates, he left the *Adventures of Huckleberry Finn* on the shelf in Key West. Instead he took *Innocents Abroad*. Together with *A Moveable Feast*, that is plenty to say grace over. He took a lot of travel books and memoirs with him, for he fully intended, as he told Janet Flanner in 1933, to write his own Paris memoirs. He also took a lot of poetrey. The thirty-year inventory shows 136 poetry entries. Now that we have his own poetry in print, the question is why wasn't it better for all his reading. Wrong question. Look, rather, at his prose, for that is where the poetry reading is important. So many of the holograph revisions were not a matter of content, but of style. Hemingway's major poetry has been in print for a long time.

There remain to be studied the literary relationships between Hemingway and his contemporaries: Joyce, Pound, Stein, Dos Passos, MacLeish, Fitzgerald, and Eliot. They are all in his reading, all in depth. No one yet has explained to us the influence of Joyce's *Dubliners* on the Hemingway short story. We have, instead, source studies, obscure, erudite, and largely improbable. The obvious studies we have side stepped. We still do not know the details of Gertrude Stein's instruction to the young Hemingway. On the basis of letters, manuscripts and published work, I think I am about to put that puzzle back together. Part of the solution is in the Stein Collection at Yale. In the Hemingway manuscripts there are scattered imitations and satires of Gertrude, which show how quickly he learned, and how the story ended. At the conclusion of one fragment, Hemingway tells us:

> Gertrude Stein was never crazy.
> Gertrude Stein was very lazy.
> Now that it is all over perhaps it made a great difference
> if it was something that you cared about. (Item 622a)

In spite of all the later animosity, Hemingway did care. Eventually we will know just how much.

Then there is Eliot whom we haven't seriously considered. We know what Hemingway said about him in the 1924 Conrad obituary, but that was merely a literary remark. I assure you that Hemingway knew his Eliot—not just the poetry, but also the essays. He thought them valuable enough to take to Cuba. Eliot allusions are scattered through the manuscripts. Eliot's objective correlative and Hemingway's the-way-it-was are different expressions of the same idea. From Eliot and Pound, Hemingway learned about Dante. Eliot's Dante study went with him to Cuba. Maybe, just maybe, Hemingway knew more Dante than most of us. Maybe Cantwell was serious when he told Renata: "I am Mister Dante. For the moment" (*Across the River*, p. 246).

In that crash-reading course that was Paris, Hemingway was bombarded with books, books urged on him by Pound, by Stein, by Sylvia Beach. The other bright young men came to Paris already sporting their college degrees. Hemingway started out behind in the course but caught up fast, outread them all. Maybe even outread Pound. Certainly outread Stein. (Just look at her checkout list from Shakespeare and Co. for a real disappointment.) The one author he could not avoid from his instructors was Henry James. Hadley loved James. Gertrude wanted to be the female Henry James of her time. Ezra, who wrote what may be his longest essay on James, gave Hemingway a recommended list of the better James. Ford Madox Ford told Hemingway anecdotes about the proper Bostonian, one censored form of which reappeared in *The Sun Also Rises*. In 1930, when Hemingway was hospitalized in Billings, Montana, Pauline read him James. And, of course, everyone was writing "A Portrait of a Lady"—Eliot, Pound, and yes, Hemingway, whose unpublished "Portrait of a Lady" is of Gertrude Stein. My inventory of the reading does not contain all of Hemingway's James reading, but a closer look at Pound's essay will provide the clues we need. Just where this line of development leads, I'm not sure. I don't know enough about James. In fact, my early reading of Hemingway was a reaction against James. But now I am certain we must return to him if we are to understand Hemingway's development. The signs of the influence will likely run beneath the surface. Carlos Baker told us that "Hemingway's doctrine of 'imitation' is of a special kind. . . . what he seeks to imitate is not the texture, it is the stature of the great books and the great pictures he admires."[4] We have already seen the connection between James' American-in-Europe and Hemingway's modern treatment of that same theme. I suspect there is more to Hemingway's James than that.

As if Henry were not bad enough, there is always William James lurking furtively in the background. It was William who so impressed Stein while she was an undergraduate at the Harvard Annex. It was William who turned her toward experiments in automatic writing, experiments which her manuscripts show she never abandoned. How much of William James Hemingway got from Stein is speculative. But he did own a copy of James' *Psychology* which he valued enough to pack for Cuba. Did he read the works on pragmatism and on religious thought? I can't prove with hard evidence that he did, but I wouldn't bet that he did not. If the brothers James are running beneath the surface of Hemingway's un-Bostonian prose, then we have a great deal of work cut out for us.

The territory that lies ahead is not a wilderness. Good people have already staked out its boundaries, charted its major rivers, laid out a few good roads—roads which have been all too main traveled. The business of the next decade is to complete their work, using every tool we own, resharpening old ones, forging new ones. We need micro studies and macro studies. We need definitive work that will finally explain *In Our Time*—take into account manuscript revisions, development of style, printing history, editorial correspondence, the relationship between the interfaces and the stories, and finally the arrangement of the stories themselves. We need wider studies as well. For all the currency of the cliché, no one has yet spelled out Hemingway's influence on twentieth-century American prose. No one has yet looked at Hemingway's economic relationship with Scribner's publishing house, the financial data for which is well preserved in New York, Princeton, and here at the Kennedy. Wider studies yet are waiting in the territory. One that I would like to read is called "The Masked Men," a book exploring the public roles that American authors create for themselves. Hemingway is a major part of that book.

To complete the necessary work, we must relearn our trade. We are not psychoanalysts, nor are we society columnists. For too long we have been blinded by scandals and feuds, by memoirs and hearsay. For too long we have not looked sufficiently beneath the surface to pursue the difficult questions. Let us here declare a moratorium on nostalgia: the Dôme cafe, Duff Twysden, all that public parade. Let us put aside those burning questions of Margot Macomber's marksmanship and the symbolism of Kilimanjaro. Let us do well what best becomes a scholar. We have manuscripts, letters, reading lists, biography, and texts. We have the territory and a few good maps, maps which still have blank spaces: unexplored regions. Starting from the measured benchmarks, we, like Eliot's old men, must become explorers.[5]

NOTES

1 Hemingway to Horace Liveright, 7 Dec. 1925.
2 Carlos Baker, *Hemingway: The Writer as Artist*, 4th ed. (Princeton: Princeton Univ. Press, 1972), p. 273.
3 Fitzgerald to Perkins, 20 Nov. 1934, in *Dear Scott/Dear Max*, edited by John Kuehl and Jackson R. Bryer (New York: Scribner's, 1971).
4 Baker, *Writer as Artist*, pp. 185-86.
5 Portions of this paper have appeared in slightly altered form in *Hemingway's Reading 1910-1940* (Princeton University Press, 1980).

"DEAR FOLKS . . . . DEAR EZRA":
HEMINGWAY'S EARLY YEARS AND CORRESPONDENCE,
1917-1924

E. R. Hagemann

The two primary sources for this article are housed in The Lilly Library, Indiana University, Bloomington—The Hemingway Letters and Manuscripts, numbering sixty-three, purchased from Mrs. Madelaine (Sunny) Hemingway Miller in Spring 1979; and The Hemingway-to-Pound Letters, numbering fourteen, written from 1922 to 1924, in the William Bird Collection. I also examined seven Pound-to-Hemingway letters, one from Dorothy Pound, and one from Bird, in the Hemingway Collection at the John F. Kennedy Library. From what has already come to be known as the Sunny Collection, I used fourteen letters written from 1917 through 1918.

With certain exceptions, these letters were not utilized by Professor Carlos Baker in *Ernest Hemingway: A Life Story* (1969). Therefore, based on this fact alone, my major premise is that emendations, additions, and reconsiderations are desirable in the Hemingway record; and I, for one, respectfully urge Professor Baker to revise the biography after he has completed the monumental task of editing the collected letters. Heaven only knows what he will have uncovered by then.

In no way do I detract from *A Life Story*. No one with sense would be so stupid. It is a major achievement in American letters. A combination of restrictions, circumstances, and happenstances prevented Professor Baker from seeing some letters. The "story" is that ordinary. Nonetheless, new data are now available, as I indicate in this paper.

The wartime letters supplement and support certain passages in Professor Michael S. Reynolds' *Hemingway's First War: The Making of "A Farewell to Arms"* (1976) and Professor Bernard Oldsey's *Hemingway's Hidden Craft: The Writing of A Farewell to Arms* (1979). Both are splendid studies.

My article is in two sections: I. Kansas City, Paris, and Milan, in which I use the Sunny Letters; II. Ernest and Ezra, in which I use the letters to Pound. The method is biographical-historical as well as interpretative.

Along with my acknowledgements, a calendar of letters is appended; some of these are difficult to date accurately.

I. *Kansas City, Paris, and Milan*

Three letters only from Hemingway's cub-reporter days in Kansas City survive in the Sunny Collection in The Lilly Library; written to his family, they are nonetheless rich in biographical and professional information. We now know, for example, that he served in the Missouri National Guard (dates to be established). More important, the letters reveal three hitherto unknown stories written by him: "Have Plenty of Coal Now" (3 December 1917, *Star*), "Note Hints at Suicide" (5 December 1917, *Times*), and "Fire Destroys Three Firms" (26 January 1918, *Star*). In his letter of 6 December, Ernest enclosed two clippings but unfortunately they no longer exist. However, recent perusal of the *Star* suggests two additional (and possible) stories, but they need to be verified.

It is well known that Ernest left the *Star* in the Spring of 1918 to join the American Red Cross Ambulance Service. He arrived in Paris early in June and from there he wrote to his family a "gee-whiz, golly-gee" letter describing both his sightseeing—Champs Élysées, Tuilleries, Louvre, the usual places one went to—and his fascination with the sporadic Big-Bertha shelling the Germans were conducting at the time. He would depart for Milan on the morrow and in one last fling, he went to the Folies Bergére. Oh, I thought when I read this, he saw Gaby Deslys and Harry Pilcer dance there—which would account for the reference in "A Way You'll Never Be." I was wrong I learned later when I read *Le Matin*. The dance team was not entertaining in June.

[Hemingway was wounded on the night of 8 July 1918, and the remainder of this section concerns his letters from the hospital] It is impossible to realize, now, that he ever wrote them, so eager are they, so patriotic. In no way do they adumbrate his fiction. But he was young and the juices were surging. He accepted without so much as a whimper everything that came his way; what did not, he sought out. In a word, the war was a game. He boasted that he had a charmed life in the trenches. He brashly told his Mother that while he was up there he had managed "to strike several slight blows towards discouraging the Austrians" and that he had glimpsed "large gobs of history" during the "great battle of the Piave" (29 July 1918). When he got word that a highschool chum had fallen in France, he hoped God would give him a chance "at some of the German swine that killed him" (7 August).

/ His admiration for the Italian troops was unbounded/ They were, he told his folks, "the bravest . . . in the Allied Armies! The mountain country is almost impossible . . . and yet they fight" (1 November 1918). They were great and he loved them (11 November 1918)/ Admiration was mutual and the Italian command awarded him three combat medals, among them the *Croce di Guerra*/ He was duly proud and in his Armistice-Day letter he drew sketches of the ribbons and designated their colors. He was getting quite "a railroad track" but he was somewhat embarrassed: he had more than some Italian officers who had been out for three years. Nowhere does he even imply that he had the medals because he was an American, as does the boy in "In Another Country."

Naturally enough, Hemingway's grave wounds—227 of them—occupy a major portion of his wartime letters. The amazing thing is this: he never admitted to any depression, any combat fatigue, although he did once grumble that he was tired of being bedridden, a month after he was hit. Without fail, he was boyishly enthusiastic. He had brushed what he euphemistically called The Great Adventure. On 18 August he drew, to exact size and shape, two mortar fragments extracted from his legs.

Recuperation and rehabilitation were long and tedious. "My left leg is all healed up and I can bend it finely and I now get around . . . on crutches. But I can only go a little bit at a time because I'm awfully weak yet" (29 August 1918) He had utter confidence in his surgeon, Captain Sammarelli, "the best in Milan." In his Armistice-Day letter, he spoke of the "machines . . . especially designed for the remaking of us mutilatis." They did wonders. Nothing like them in the States. After another six weeks, his leg would be practically as good as ever, "a fine workmanlike leg," he said. One can but remark at the startling difference between Ernest and the wounded boy in "In Another Country."

I do not exaggerate when I say that Hemingway enjoyed his hospital tour of duty. He welcomed visitors and the Americans in Milan were, he said, "indescribably nice" and fetched him books, cakes, and candy. An Englishman "adopted" him and shared the London papers; a "peach" of a Catholic missionary priest was often there for "great old gab fests," as were his "jolly good Italian officer pals"—and suddenly we are amidst Chapters 11 and 12 of *A Farewell to Arms*. He brags about his fluency in Italian, his grasp of French, and his smidgin of Polish. He promised his family that there wouldn't be "any such thing" as foreigners for him after the War. "That's the best thing about this mess, the friends that it makes." When one looked at death, he said, one got to know one's friends (29 August 1918). He mentioned the wonderful American nurses and told Mother he was in love (he never revealed the identity of Agnes von Kurowsky) but not for her to get "the wind up and start worrying" about marriage. Mother Grace was still his "best girl" (29 August 1918).

He loved Milan—"a peach of a town" with its beautiful Cathedral. He could see the dome from the hospital-porch and he admired the interior and the columns that went "way up in the sky" (29 July 1918). He went to *La Scala* and one time he heard Toscanini direct Arrigo Boito's *Mefistofele*, but he preferred *Carmen*. He got to know some of the singers who hung around the American Bar. Once again—foreshadowings of *Farewell*—Ralph Simmons and others (Chapter 19).

In late September, he took a ten-day leave from the hospital and went up to Stresa on Lago Maggiore. On his second night there, he met centenarian

Count Giuseppe Greppi who introduced him "to about 150 people." Ernest
was impressed. "He is perfectly preserved, has never married, goes to bed at
midnight and smokes and drinks champagne" (29 September 1918). The
elegant Count regaled his young friend with tales of his *amori* and a *vignetta*
about dining with Maria Luisa, Napoleon's second wife, in Vienna in the
1840s. I yearned for Hemingway to recount their billiards, but he didn't.
That was reserved for *Farewell* (Chapter 35).

"In the fall the war was always there but we did not go to it any more,"
goes the first sentence of "In Another Country." Well, Hemingway did
once more and paid for it. He contrived a leave from the hospital on 24
October 1918, the day the Vittorio-Veneto offensive shoved off, and made
for the front. "Worked hard day and night where the worst mountain fighting was and then came down with jaundice. It makes you feel rotten . . . but
is nothing to worry about," he assured his Family on 1 November. Ten days
later it was all cleared up, a remarkable recovery indeed. His account sharply differs from that of Carlos Baker in *Life Story* who says that Ernest was
stricken the day after the offensive started. The matter needs looking into. I
don't think Hemingway exaggerated; Baker does.

Actually, Hemingway returned to the war zone yet again, but when it was
all over. On 7 December he drove to Torreglia to visit some British artillery
officers; two days later, with a friend, he was in Treviso see "the girl," as he
guardedly referred to Agnes, who was in a field hospital. Their party of
four—Agnes, Ernest, Lt. Hey, and Nurse Smith—went all over the battle-
field and saw the old Austrian trenches and "the mined houses of Nervesa
by moonlight and searchlight. It was a great trip" (11 December 1918).

He was restless and wondered what he would do, now that the War was
over. As early as late September he had doubts. "Gee I'm afraid I won't be
good for anything after this war! All I know now is war! Everything else
seems like a dream." He was in no hurry to hustle back to Oak Park. He
had vague notions of seeing Austria and Italy. A wealthy family he had met
at Stresa invited him to Turin; another invitation was to come down to
Abruzzi for shooting and pigsticking; his CO, Captain Gamble, proposed
visiting Madeira for two months. Ernest thought he might go to Trieste.
Nothing worked out except the jaunt to see Agnes; he did not mention
journeying to Taormino (Sicily), which both Baker and Reynolds bring up.

Finally, on 11 December, he notified his Folks he would sail from Genoa
on 4 January and be in Oak Park later that month. He had discarded the
idea of bumming around. "I was made to be one of those beastly writing
chaps y' know . . . the Lord neglected to have me born with money—so I've
got to work to make it and the sooner the better." At age nineteen and a
half he has decided to become a writer. A month earlier, he had vowed that
when he did return, he would commence "the real war again. The war to
make the world safe for Ernie Hemingway." One thing was clear: Oak Park

was farther away than mere geography. Too much had happened. Harold Krebs found his "Soldier's Home" impossible. Whether he knew it or not, Tenente Ernest M. Hemingway was Krebs.

II. Ernest and Ezra

Hemingway's letters to Pound were informal, composed without "history" lurking over his shoulder. He was writing to a friend, fourteen years his senior, and was himself. He often commented on his work and his writing. He loved to gossip and so did Ezra. He was, at times, meanspirited and his anti-Semitism was too apparent for comfort. He was gorgeously profane. For some reason the verb "bugger" and the noun "shit," the latter applied to anyone he disliked, fascinated him. He was not above a pun and idiosyncratic spelling, both, I imagine, picked up from Pound. His affection for his friend approached worship, tinged with awe. If he was not Ezra, he was "Duce," "Carino," "Esteemed General" (Ernest was "Colonel Hemingway"), and "Prometheus." He longed for Pound when he was absent and said so outright. Pound, as befitted seniority, was reserved and eschewed intimacy; he called Hemingway "Hem" but always signed "E" or "E.P." Ernest never used any cognomen but "Hem." Both he and Hadley adored Dorothy Pound as she did them. Hadley is occasionally spoken of but never disparagingly, even after the loss of the precious manuscripts.

In short, Hemingway was gratified by the fact that the elder writer had early on recognized the worth of his writing and understood at once what he was up to. Pound was the first, possibly the *only*, man Hemingway ever knew whom he could confide in, drink with, and share with his craft. Therefore, the Hem-Ezra letters, amounting to some 8500 words, considerably expand upon the relationship as described by Carlos Baker.

In the first extant letter, written in late Spring 1922, Ernest said he knew what *he* was after in prose and hoped to give Pound a couple of samples in six months. If it was "no fucking good," he'd know it and praise by Lincoln Steffens and such—he rattled out a dazzling list of names—would cut "no bloody ice." He thanked Pound for including him in the "Inquest into the State of Contemporary English Prose" (his contribution would be the sixth) to be issued by William Bird at Three Mountains Press, and he promised not to "detonate" if Pound regretted having "publicly backed some one" whom he now realized had "nothing worth printing" and wanted "to yank out of the sextette." Erza had no such intention despite having known Ernest but two months at the most.

In December 1922, in a Paris *gare*, Hadley had a valise stolen which contained her husband's manuscripts. He was at Chamby sur Montreux and did not report the loss to Pound for almost a month, 23 January 1923. (His immediate account does not square with *A Moveable Feast* nor does it square with Baker's *Life Story*.) Last week, he told Ezra, he went up to

Paris "to see what was left and found that Hadley had made the job complete by including all carbons, duplicates, etc." Some incidental correspondence remained. "You, naturally, would say, 'Good' etc. But don't say it to me. I ain't reached that mood. I worked 3 years on the damn stuff. Some like Paris 1922 I fancied." But he was working again on some "new stuff" and had six months' "grub money ahead."

Pound's handwritten response, postmarked 27 January 1923 at Rapallo, was instructive, gruffly sympathetic. "I never said the loss of your juvernalia was a blessing. "It's possibly a calamity—certainly damn'd annoying. . . . In the long run . . . nobody is *known* to have lost anything by *suppression* of early work. But that ain't the same thing. The *point is*: how much of *it can you remember*. What you are *out* of pocket is the *time* it will . . . take you . . . to rewrite the parts you can remember. . . . If the middle, i.e., *FORM*, of a story is right one ought to be able to reassemble it from memory. . . . As has been remarked: memory is the best critic. If the thing wobbles and won't reform then it has no proper construction, and never *wd.* have been *right*. All of which is probably cold comfort." Hemingway's reaction two days later was a sarcastic marginal note: he thanked Carino for "advice to a young man on the occasion of the loss by stealing of his complete works." He promised to "foller" the advice. I believe he did—he never again spoke of the loss.

That Summer he was carefully organizing and polishing the vignettes that would constitute *in our time*. In early August he wrote of his progress. (The numerals refer to those in the 1924 edition.) He would redo "the hanging" (17); he had redone Maera's death (16) and "fixed" the others. Each one should be headed "Chapter 1, Chapter 2, etc. When they are read altogether they all hook up." It seemed "funny" but they did. The bulls started, then reappeared, then finished off (2, 12-16). The war started "clear and noble just like it did" (4-5), got close and blurred (1, 7-8), and finished with the "feller" who went home and got "the clap" (10). The refugees left Thrace (3), due to the Greek ministers who were shot (6). The whole thing closed with the Greek King and Queen in the garden (18). The radicals started noble with the young Magyar (11) and then got "bitched." America appeared "in the cops shooting the guys who robbed the cigar store" (9). It had *form*, all right!

Comments are called for: (1) Hemingway's intriguing arrangement was not followed; (2) the word "bitched" signifies another radical chapter, other than Ten (originally titled "Youth").

Shortly after this letter was posted, Ernest and Hadley went to Toronto to await the birth of their first child. Meanwhile, Bird, who was in Venice, arrived at an elaborate design and format for *in our time*. He wrote Pound about "framing each page . . . in a border of newspaper print," carefully selecting for both decoration and illustration. For example, "the bull fight chapters framed with cuttings from Bullfight journals,'' etc. He attached a sketch of Chapter 10 to show what he meant (17 September 1923). Pound proposed, apparently, sending the sketch and the letter to Hem for approval or disapproval. Bird agreed, more or less, mostly less.

Hemingway, taken up with Bumby's arrival, delayed writing Ezra until about 13 October. He said he had cabled Bird "to commence firing on the newsprint borders," but it would all depend "on how it was done." A good "hunch," however, and Bill was "the man to do it." If not well done, it would "sour quick as hell." As it turned out, Bird dropped his plans. The remnants are today to be seen in the headline-collages on the front and back covers of the 1924 edition which was delayed and Hemingway, back in Paris, was miffed. "After awaiting various dates," he had lost the "the fine thrill enjoyed by Benj. Franklin when entering Philadelphia with a roll under each arm." He unleased an imprecation: "Fuck Literature!" (17 March 1924).

He had loathed, despised Toronto and North America and everything and every place west of the Seine. Nothing was right; all was wrong in Exile. To capstone his troubles, he was overworked by the *Star*. Such dirges the like of his have probably never been chanted on the north shore of Lake Ontario. "It couldn't be worse. You can't imagine it" (6 September 1923). He couldn't sleep "just with the horror of the Goddamn thing." He hadn't had a drink in five days. The previous night he lay awake reading *Ulysses* to cheer him up. "Write me—you may save a human life," he wailed. In October his rage reached break-point. He was on assignment when Hadley was in labor, and he stormed into his city editor's office intent upon homicide. He compromised: henceforth, all work would be done with the upmost contempt for Harry Hindmarsh and "his bunch of masturbating mouthed associates!" Little wonder his job was "highly insecure." He couldn't buy candy for Hadley in hospital because candy, mind you, was forbidden to be sold in Toronto on Sunday! No doubt about it—Canada was "the fistulated asshole of the father of seven among Nations." His stomach was shot "from nervous fatigue."

His one thought, his obsession, was to return to Paris and see Ezra whom he prayed would await him. "Christ," he said, how he wanted to get "drunk with some one that knew what the hell he was talking about." Prometheus was right: it was all right to do it once—come back—but better yet, not to have done it at all (9 December 1923). He dreamt of throwing a party at Canneton's in Paris, if Pound would only stay. He climaxed his tirade, somewhat incoherently, with a roll call of shits that is absolutely Homeric in scope, then perorated triumphantly: "*Shit on them all*." Poor Pound! He had not yet received this epistolary marvel when he wrote on 17 December and in a rather businesslike manner offered his apartment-studio at 70 *bis* rue-Notre-Dame-des-Champs to the three of them. He was leaving Paris on

5 January. Because of the baby, Hemingway decided against Nr. 70. Instead, he moved his family in down the street at Nr. 113.

One time in 1924, he made a joke about the address and called it rue-Notre-Dame-des-*Champions*. But was he joking? I think not. Now that *in our time* was out, he regarded himself as a Champion along with Pound; thus, the plural noun. His literary combativeness matched his combativeness in the ring—we must remember he was a boxer—and in war. He was particularly touchy about his attainments in prose; which is to say, he saw himself as an original, not a deriver, and he resented critics, *et al.*, suggesting otherwise. He reacted strongly to Lewis Galantière's article in the Paris *Chicago Tribune* and exasperatingly complained that the man set out to prove that "the mantle of Abe Lincoln, Wm. Dean Howells, Hamlin Garland, Sherwood Anderson and Yourself" was descending upon him (early May 1924). In July he griped bitterly about Burton Rascoe's remark that *in our time* showed "the influence of who the hell do you think?—Ring Lardner and Sherwood Anderson!" In this same letter, by some arcane reasoning, he stated his conviction that Ford Madox Ford had killed his chances to have a book published in the Fall of that year. "By next Spring, some son of a bitch will have copied everything I've written and they will simply call me another of his imitators." He felt cheerful as hell. Ezra was "the only guy" who knew "a god damn thing about writing."

And the only one of his Parisian compeers Hemingway truly respected. Lincoln Steffens was "a sweet old man." T. S. Eliot should "strangle his sick wife, bugger the brain specialist and rob the bank"; then he might write "an even better poem." About Robert McAlmon, who had published *Three Stories and Ten Poems* in the Summer of 1923, he had mixed feelings. George Antheil, the *avant-garde* American composer, was "an excellent lad." *The Dial*, its staff and contributors were contemptible. "The dial have given their 2,000 paper ones," he gossiped, "to Wickham Brooks or Van Wyck Steed or somebody" (10 February 1924). *Broom* was another target.

As was James Joyce, even though Hemingway, at one time, had had high regard for *Ulysses*—as we have seen. In July 1924, having seen the *corridas* in Pamplona, he told Ezra that the Plaza in the afternoon was the only "remaining place where valor and art" could combine for success. In all other arts, "the more meazly and shitty the guy," Joyce, for example, the greater his success in his art. There was absolutely no comparison between Joyce and Maera, the *matador de toros*. "Maera by a mile." Look at the two of them. One bred Georgios! The other either got killed or bred bulls!

Because Hemingway had worked for Ford Madox Ford on *transatlantic review* and been around him for some time, he knew FMF better than anyone except Pound. Ernest had his troubles with the man. Ford could explain "stuff . . . but in private life" he was so involved "in being the dregs of an

English country gentleman" that no one could get any "good out of him." Ford never recovered "in a literary way from the miracle . . . of his having been a soldier. Down with gentlemen. They're hell on themselves in literature" (17 March 1924). Oddly, Hemingway liked the Briton. But he was not doing enough for writing in the *review*. He ran it as compromise. Anything he accepted and published could just as easily have been published in *Harper's* or *Century* "except Tzara and such shit in French." "That's the hell of it." Goddamn it, Ernest fumed, he didn't have any advertisers to "offend" or any subscribers to "discontinue." "Why not shoot the moon?" If you think some of this has a familiar ring, then you remember the chapter devoted to Ford in *A Moveable Feast*.

There is more raillery in the letters but—

Hemingway had come a long, long way since January 1919 when he sailed for home. He was what he had wanted to be: a writer— and a writer of extraordinary merit. In June 1918, he was a sightseer in Paris; in 1924, he was a denizen of the 6^e Arrondissement and the city, the city, as he said in *Feast*, to which "there is never any ending."

ACKNOWLEDGEMENTS

In the way of acknowledgements, I thank Miss Saundra Taylor, Curator of Manuscripts, The Lilly Library; Mr. William Cagle, Librarian, The Lilly Library; Miss Jo August, Curator of the Hemingway Collection, John F. Kennedy Library; and their staffs for help in this project. I also cite a small grant from the Research Committee, College of Arts and Sciences, University of Louisville.

I appreciate the kindness of Mr. James Laughlin, Norfolk, Connecticut, who allowed me to quote from one of Pound's letters; especially do I appreciate the kindness of Mr. Alfred Rice, attorney-at-law, New York City, who, representing the Hemingway Estate, gave permission to quote from all Hemingway letters. And above all, I express my gratitude to Mr. Charles Scribner, Jr. for his interest in this article.

CALENDAR OF LETTERS

Part I: Kansas City, Paris, and Milan

6 December 1917. EMH to Family. Kansas City. 2 leaves; 3 pages. TL. [Date not in EH's hand.]

30 January 1918. EMH to Family. Kansas City. 2 leaves; 3 pages. TLS; signed in pencil. [Date not in EH's hand.]

12 February 1918. EMH to Grandmother (Adelaide Edmunds Hemingway). Kansas City. 1 leaf; 1 page. TLS; signed in pencil.

3(?) June 1918. EMH to Family (?). Paris. 2 leaves; 2 pages of 3; page 1 missing; YMCA stationery. ALS; ink. [Note on verso, page 3, not in EH's hand.]

29 July 1918. EMH to Mother. Milan; A.R.C. Hospital. 2 leaves; 8 pages. ALS; ink. [EH misnumbered last page as "9."]

7 August 1918. EMH to Family. Milan. 2 leaves; 4 pages; A.R.C. stationery. ALS; ink.

18 August 1918. EMH to Family. Milan; A.R.C. Hospital. 4 leaves; 7 pages. ALS; ink. [Note on verso, page 7, in EH's hand and directed to Father.]

29 August 1918. EMH to Mother. Milan; A.R.C. Hospital. 2 leaves; 6 pages. ALS; ink. [Postmarked 28 August 1918.]

26 September 1918. EMH to Father. Stresa. Postcard. ALS; pencil.

29 September 1918. EMH to Family. Stresa. 3 leaves; 6 pages. ALS; ink(?).

1 November 1918. EMH to Family. Milan; A.R.C. Hospital. 1 leaf; 2 pages. ALS; ink.

11 November 1918. EMH to Family. Milan; A.R.C. Hospital. 3 leaves; 6 pages. ALS; ink. [Page 3 has sketches by EH of his ribbons.]

14 November 1918. EMH to Father. Milan; A.R.C. Hospital. 2 leaves; 4 pages. ALS; ink.

28 November 1918. EMH to Family. Milan. 2 leaves; 4 pages. ALS; ink. [Written Thanksgiving night.]

11 December 1918. EMH to Family. Milan. 3 leaves; 3 pages. ALS; red ink. [Year not in EH's hand.]

The above letters are in The Lilly Library, Indiana University.

Part II: Ernest and Ezra

Late Spring (?) 1922. EMH to EP. Paris. 2 leaves; 3 pages. ALS; pencil.

31 August 1922 [postmarked]. EMH to EP. Triberg. Postcard. ALS; pencil.

23 January 1923. EMH to EP. Chamby sur Montreux. 2 leaves; 2 pages. ALS; pencil.

*27 January 1923 [postmarked]. EP to EMH. Ripallo. 4 leaves; 4 pages. ALS; ink.

29 January 1923. EMH to EP. Chamby sur Montreux. 2 leaves; 2 pages. TL.

10 March 1923. EMH to EP. Milan. 1 leaf; 1 page. TL. [On verso, note in EP's hand to William Bird; ink.]

Early August (?) 1923. EMH to EP. Paris. 1 leaf; 1 page. TL. [Undated; no envelope.]

6(?) September 1923. EMH to EP. Toronto. 2 leaves; 2 pages. TL.

*21 September 1923. EP to EMH. Paris. 3 leaves; 3 pages. TLS; date and initial "E" in EP's hand.

23 September 1923. EMH to EP. Toronto. 1 leaf; 2 pages. TLS; signed in pencil.

*25 September 1923. EP to EMH; scrawled note, signed "E," to forward ALS from William Bird to EP. Venice; dated 17 September 1923.

*October (?) 1923. EP to EMH. Paris. 1 leaf; 1 page. TL. [Note in EP's hand at bottom of page.]

13(?) October 1923. EMH to EP. Toronto. 2 leaves; 2 pages. TL. [Verso, page 2, has typed note from EMH.]

*24 October 1923. EP to EMH. Paris. 3 leaves; 3 pages. TLS; signed "E."

9 December 1923. EMH to EP. Toronto. 10 leaves; 10 pages. ALS; ink. [Written on Postal Telegraph forms.]

*17 December 1923. EP to EMH. Paris. 1 leaf; 1 page. TLS; signed "E.P."

*22 December 1923. DP to EMH. Paris. 2 leaves; 2 pages. ALS; ink.

10 February 1924. EMH to EP. Paris. 4 leaves; 4 pages. ALS; ink. [Scrambled notes on verso, page 4.]

17 March 1924. EMH to EP. Paris. 3 leaves; 6 pages. ALS; ink.

2(?) May 1924. EMH to EP. Paris. 5 leaves; 8 pages. ALS; pencil.

*10 June 1924 [postmarked]. EP to EMH. Paris. 1 leaf; 1 page. TL. [Note in EP's hand on verso of envelope.]

19 July 1924. EMH to EP. Burguete. 2 leaves; 4 pages. ALS; ink.

The letters marked with an asterisk are in the John F. Kennedy Library; the other letters are in The Lilly Library.

HEMINGWAY'S BEGINNINGS AND ENDINGS

Bernard Oldsey

The manuscripts in the Hemingway Collection have two remarkable and almost contradictory characteristics. One is the free-flowing and finished quality of the prose that makes up most of the interior passages of the stories and novels. There are some emendations and reworkings of these passages, and in some instances the changes do provide insight into the author's method and meaning; but the remarkable thing is that there are so few of these, relatively speaking, and that the interior prose runs on so smoothly and ineluctably for such long stretches at a time.

The other striking feature of the manuscripts—and one that is much more rewarding critically—manifests itself in the numerous drafts and emendations of beginnings and endings done for both the short stories and the novels. These do not, of course, signal strange or unusual difficulties peculiar to Hemingway. Anybody who has ever written anything will understand why this is so: as George Eliot once confided in correspondence, "Beginnings are always troublesome" and "conclusions are the weak point of most authors." What is unusual, and critically gratifying, is that Hemingway left behind such an abundance of evidence showing how a writer overcomes these difficulties.

From this evidence emerges a pattern of writing and rewriting, vision and revision, that transforms raw material into finished art. The manuscripts show that Hemingway was not only a great natural writer, possessed of verve and linguistic flow, but also a fine editor of his own fiction. His sense of what was right, what would work, was uncanny. The papers reveal that he made very few, if any, incorrect decisions about how to begin or end a narrative. In this respect, Ezra Pound's irreverent summation of Hemingway's talent is not inappropriate: "The son of a bitch's *instincts* are right!"

Even in those rare instances where the record indicates that outside advice was offered, Hemingway chose wisely which advice to accept and which to reject. He did, as we now know, accept F. Scott Fitzgerald's advice on how to begin *The Sun Also Rises*. At various stages of development it began with Brett Ashley, Jake Barnes, with Niño de Palma; but then because of Fitzgerald's advice, Hemingway cut deeply into the early drafts and started with Robert Cohn, thereby ridding the book of much useless stuff. As treated by Philip Young and Charles Mann, this instance became, quite rightly, a rather famous case of modern literary influence.[1] But later, with the Hemingway papers more readily and fully available, it was discovered that the influ-

ence-ledger was in need of some balancing. As indicated in a recent study
(*Hemingway's Hidden Craft*, 1979) Hemingway rejected a number of Fitzgerald's suggestions about the composition of *A Farewell to Arms*, including one about how to conclude the novel; and subsequently, Fitzgerald
fashioned the ending of his own *Tender is the Night* on the basis of something that he learned from Hemingway, something that came out of the
"troubles with the very end of *A Farewell to Arms.*"[2]

Hemingway's Hidden Craft discusses these troubles—examining and
codifying forty-one concluding attempts for the novel, including clusters of
variants like "The *Nada* Ending," "The Fitzgerald Ending," "The Religious Ending," "The Live-Baby Ending," "The Morning-After Ending,"
"The Funeral Ending," "The Original *Scribner's Magazine* Ending," as
well as five versions of "*The* Ending," as published. These revisions depict
the story behind the story, detailing how Hemingway finally arrived at the
flat, nihilistic, numbing conclusion that the novel now has.[3]

This study also discusses what is probably the original beginning of *A
Farewell to Arms* (Item 240 in the papers). Consisting of two chapters, the
early manuscript starts at a point roughly equivalent to Chapter XIII (the
first chapter of Book Two) of the novel as published. In one of the few instances to be found in the papers, Hemingway here reversed his usual method of arriving at a true beginning by cutting: here he added twelve chapters
of vital plot and character introduction to the original beginning—in which
the already wounded protagonist (named Emmett Hancock) is being carried
to a room in a hospital in Milan. One important result of this recasting is
that the novel now opens with its celebrated lyrical overture instead of a secondary action *in medias res.*[4]

The opening and closing variants of *A Farewell to Arms* may well be
among the most dramatic and revealing changes to be found in the Hemingway manuscripts; but they have been fully discussed elsewhere, and they are
by no means unique in their ability to reflect Hemingway's editorial perception and narrative craftsmanship. So it is the intent of this present analysis
to concentrate on the manuscripts of three other works—three representative short stories that underwent radical beginning and/or ending changes
and were thus transformed into remarkably different works from those
originally intended. Examining these stories should demonstrate the kind of
critical information that resides within the boxed manuscripts. An Alad-
din's rub may summon forth nothing more than testimony that reinforces
previous readings and opinions of these works; or it may, in producing a
clearer picture of Hemingway at work, clarify technical and thematic aspects of his fiction that cannot be perceived by reading it only in final form.

I. "Indian Camp"

One of the manuscripts chosen for examination here is Item 493, the earliest extant version of "Indian Camp." This is, of course, a key work in the Hemingway canon: the first of the Nick Adams stories, both in publication and in the chronology of this cycle, it is also a typical *tranche de vie*, done as Hemingway most often did these pieces, from a third-person-singular point of view, with touches of omniscient adjustment. Furthermore, most of this manuscript has been made public, and it contains an example of a particular kind of auctorial epiphany that characterizes much of Hemingway's work.

The story as published (in *Transatlantic Review*, April 1924, under the indicative heading of "Work in Progress") opens with the line "At the lake shore there was another row boat drawn up."[5] In manuscript, this line does not appear until p. 9. The previous eight pages, published with slight changes as "Three Shots" in *The Nick Adams Stories* (1972), constitute a small flashback, recounting the events of the previous evening: Nick has accompanied his father and his Uncle George (Uncle *Joe* in the first, rejected paragraph of the manuscript) on a camping-fishing trip; and what he remembers is that on the evening before, left behind in camp while his father and uncle go off to fish by jacklight, he behaved in a cowardly manner. (Later, in writing "The Short Happy Life of Francis Macomber," Hemingway would use much the same method of beginning, with a flashback to an act of cowardice. And as we shall see, he had to make as drastic a change to get Macomber's story properly started as he did in this instance with Nick's.)

According to Julian Smith, excision of the first eight pages from "Indian Camp" was nothing more than "the kind of editorial cut many authors make without greatly altering the effect or meaning of a story."[6] But in making this statement Smith proves to be the critical victim of not knowing; and his article on "Hemingway and the Thing Left Out," which is basically a good one, stands as an example of previous commentary that needs revision in light of the manuscripts. The article appeared in 1971, before "Three Shots" was published; and Smith made his comment without first-hand knowledge of the manuscript, solely on the basis of a summary account provided by Carlos Baker.[7]

Actually, the initial eight pages of the manuscript shed considerable light on the central motivation and effect of "Indian Camp." Philip Young, who did have access to this material before writing " 'Big World Out There': The Nick Adams Stories," quite rightly emphasizes the change in thematic tack the story underwent.[8] In the first section of the manuscript the author had concentrated on Nick's fear of death, his realization that his own "silver cord" would be cut. The story as published retains no mention of this motivational background; instead, it moves on to a truer, more valid, kind of perception: the realization that a young boy might feel "quite sure that he would never die." As Young concludes, "children don't really believe in their own demise. Death is obviously something that happens to other people.''[9]

Young's perceptive comment indicates how knowing a manuscript can help elucidate the work as published. But the matter is psychologically and artistically more complicated than he concludes. Does the ending of the story present us with the thoughts of a child, or with those of a child becoming a man? It should be observed that the first eight pages of this manuscript do much to establish Nick Adams—even at this tender age, when his father still calls him "Nickie"—as the essential Hemingway hero, who cannot sleep nights, has fears that he may cease to be, and badly needs some kind of therapeutic device, or activity, to help him through his nocturnal anxiety. In a flashback within a flashback, Nick recalls another time when he was beset by cowardly fear: this is a night at home when "he sat out in the hall under the night light trying to read Robinson Crusoe to keep his mind off the fact that someday the silver chord [sic] must break." [10] He recognizes that this is the same kind of fear that made him poke his rifle outside the tent and fire three times, recalling his father and uncle by prearranged signal in case of emergency.

The silver-cord motif tied the entire manuscript together before Hemingway made his cut. The idea enters by way of a hymn that Nick knows from church, and in his mind it connotes death. Of course, quite literally it denotes the umbilical cord and thus the beginning of life. And in both senses it was quite fitting within the terms of the story, with the birth of the Indian child and the death of the Indian father—who severs his own lifeline by slitting his throat.

When Hemingway excised the first eight pages of the manuscript, the narrative lost its informing image, but the after-effect of this particular "thing left out" can still be sensed in the beautifully worked out conclusion of the story. And here too the manuscript is fascinatingly informative. After the life and death events of the night, Nick and his father return to their camp in a row boat. Dr. Adams answers his son's questions about the pains of birth and the pains of dying. What was to have been the last paragraph runs like this:

> They were seated in the boat, Nick in the stern his father rowing. The sun was coming up over the hills. A bass jumped making a circle in the water. Nick trailed his hand in the water. It felt warm in the sharp *shell* of the morning.[11]

In other words, Hemingway was tempted to end the story with this pretty line of imagery depicting the welcome arrival of day. Right after it he placed the journalist's mark of "30."

The two inches of manuscript between the initial "30" and the next one, which marks the end of the story as we know it, represents a quantum leap in artistic insight. For here Hemingway added that irresistibly shrugging one-sentence paragraph which gives the story so much of its concluding power: "In the early morning on the lake sitting in the stern of the boat with his father rowing he felt quite sure he would never die."[12]

How are we to read this remarkable final sentence, with its pulsing and carefully modifying prepositional phrases? Is it to be read only as an ironic indication of childish egocentrism? Another manuscript example—this from Stephen Crane's papers—may help provide an answer. For at one time Crane was tempted to conclude *The Red Badge of Courage* on a similar note of youthful self-centeredness: in an early version of the novel, he represented his protagonist, Henry Fleming, as having "been to touch the great death" and finding that "after all, it was but the great death *and was for others.*"[13] But eventually Crane removed those four final incriminating words, and in doing so allowed his young Union soldier to stand as something more than a case of arrested literary development, and the butt of the author's irony.

Hemingway did somewhat the same thing in Nick Adam's case, except that he added words in his final instance instead of removing them. And here again the papers indicate how artistically right Hemingway could be at a deep intuitive level. As he first set the concluding sentence of "Indian Camp" down on paper, it was simple, flat, and unexceptional: all it said was, "In the early morning on the lake he felt quite sure he would never die." But with the touch of a twenty-five-year-old genius, Hemingway piled on those phrases that move the sentence, circumscribe its meaning, and mitigate whatever irony it may contain.

What he finally leaves the reader with is a genre painting of transcendental potential. There in the row boat on the lake sitting safely in the stern of the boat is a youthful Nick Adams who has not quite severed the psychic umbilical cord stretching between him and his father, the master of life and death questions. His father sits before him in the boat, and all's right with the world, as a fish jumps and makes a perfect circle in the water. And yet looked at from another view, isn't the boy Nick already father of all those fictional men of Hemingway's later making? All those who have to sleep with the light on, who have to think of women they have known, streams they have fished, in order to achieve some kind of solace at night? Those who have to learn how to use the abiding beauty of the earth as something of a stay against neurotic fear and trembling?

On a day like this, within "the sharp shell of the morning," any man or child might believe that he could live forever. It may be an egocentric thought, but it is also therapeutic, and Nick Adams, age approximately fourteen, has as much right to it as all the primitive, and not so primitive, theologians and transcendentalists who have purveyed it since time immemorial. With certain elements of glory in sight, this boy about to become a man may entertain intimations of immortality as well as any grown-up

Wordsworth. And if any irony attaches, it applies to both the boy and the poet.

II. "Big Two-Hearted River"

Though they are important, even vital, the changes Hemingway made in "Indian Camp" look rather minor when compared to the major surgery he performed on another Nick Adams story called "Big Two-Hearted River," which was published a year later, in *This Quarter* (May 1925), and was used as the culminating story of *In Our Time* (also 1925). Thirty-four years later—in an unpublished introductory piece entitled "The Art of the Short Story"—Hemingway disclosed many of his theories about the writing of fiction. Some sections of this typescript are ga-ga and silly, but others are penetrating and wise, representing a series of criteria the author had worked out for himself. One of the most revealing of these statements deals with the efficacy of omission, with particular reference to "Big Two-Hearted River":

> A few things I have found to be true. If you leave out important things or events that you know about, the story is strengthened. If you leave out or skip something because you do not know it, the story will be worthless. The test of any story is how very good the stuff is that you, not your editors, omit. A story in this book called Big Two-Hearted River is about a boy coming home beat to the wide from a war. Beat to the wide was an earlier and possibly more severe form of beat, since those who had it were unable to comment on this condition and could not suffer that it be mentioned in their presence. So the war, all mention of the war, anything about the war, is omitted. The river was the Fox river, by Seney, Michigan, not the Big Two-Hearted. The change of name was made purposely, not from ignorance nor carelessness but because Big Two-Hearted River is poetry, and because there were many Indians in the story, just as the war was in the story, and none of the Indians nor the war appeared. As you see, it is very simple and easy to explain. [14]

Of course, it is not "very simple and easy to explain"; nor are the distant war and vanishing Indians the only things the author omitted from the story. By the time he wrote "The Art of the Short Story" (dated June 1959), Hemingway may have forgotten the difficulties he had had with the composition of "Big Two-Hearted River." But several manuscripts (Items 274, 275, and 279) show that he eventually changed much more than the name of the river. They indicate, in fact, that he had at least two chances to ruin the work—once before it even got properly under way, and once when it started to run out of control at the end. In both instances, the story went through a process that entailed omission of extraneous matter and a reconceputalization of the narrative structure.

The story as published begins, "The train went on up the track out of sight, around one of the hills of burnt timber." Nick Adams has just hopped off the train at the site of what had been a town. Now everything is in ruins—including all "thirteen saloons that had lined the one street of Seney," as well as the "burned-over stretch of hillside, where he expected to find the scattered houses of the town." After this quick survey of peacetime devastation, Nick immediately (in the second paragraph) sets off down the railroad track to the river he intends to fish.

Startlingly enough, the earliest manuscript fragment of the story (Item 279) begins in this way: "*They* got off the train at Seney. There was no station."[15] The reader is amazed to discover that this work—which so depends for its effect upon a solitary figure set within a physical and mental wilderness—was intially conceived with three characters in it: Nick, Jack, and Al. Continued in this fashion, this piece might well have developed into one of Hemingway's typical boon-companion scenarios (like that in "Cross-Country Snow" and in the fishing section of *The Sun Also Rises*) where men escape the consequences of civilization by fishing or skiing together in a wilderness setting. Actually, some of this scenario carried over into a later typescript version of the story (Item 275), as Nick recalls all the times he had fished with male companions, like "Bill Smith, Odgar, the Ghee, all the old gang." But now these times are over with—he realizes—because in accepting the responsibilities of marrying (*Hadley* in one version, *Helen* in another) he had admitted there was "something more important than fishing."[16]

Another feature of the fragment (Item 279) that immediately strikes the reader is the viewpoint from which it is told. Hemingway struck through the first word of this version, changing the pronoun "We" to "They." In the first instance, he would have been stuck with a first-person point of view; in the second, he committed himself to an omniscient approach—for the duration of the fragment, which runs for only three pages.

What Nick, Jack, and Al do within these three pages is something that Hemingway eventually left out. Gathering together their gear from the railroad tracks, they proceed to inspect the burnt-out town, particularly the ruins of the Mansion House Hotel. As they poke around in the basement debris, they find four gun barrels, "pitted and twisted by the heat"; and in the magazine of one gun, they discover how the "cartridges had melted" and "formed a bulge of lead and copper." The fragment stops at this point. Hemingway obviously pushed it aside as a false start and began all over again, retaining little from the fragment except the general setting and the principal character. Had he retained some of the descriptive detail, he might have reinforced an idea that some commentators have, with critical hindsight, caught a glimmer of—namely, that the initial scene of burnt pine lands and ravaged town is the peace-time equivalent of war-time devastation.[17] But since the author knew about the war and the twisted guns, knew that the foundation of the hotel was "lime stone chipped and split by fire," he could, in terms of his own theory, leave that information out of the story and strengthen it. And when, as Mark Twain might put it, he found that having Jack and Al around would prove embarrassing, he simply buried them in the basement pit of the Mansion House. For to have provided Nick with what Hemingway later called "the comforting stench of human companionship" would have ruined the entire effect of this story, which of all his works is most dependent upon a single sensibility, an almost perfectly controlled "center of intelligence," confronting itself in the wilderness.[18]

The solution Hemingway found to the problem of beginning "Big Two-Hearted River" was vital but relatively simple. Reaching a proper conclusion called for a more involved process of revision. The concluding section of the story starts about four pages from the end, where Nick just misses catching the biggest trout he "ever heard of." His struggle with the fish threatens his emotional stability: he feels "a little sick, as though it would have been better to sit down." Somewhat later he sits on a log with his feet dangling over the water. While eating some sandwiches and then smoking a cigarette, he is perfectly at ease, until he notices how the river narrows and enters a swamp. Troubled by the thought that "the fishing would be tragic" in the swamp, he decides not "to go down the stream any further today." Instead, he busies himself, killing the two trout he has caught, and cleaning them in the stream. This done, he climbs the bank of the river and walks toward the high ground and his camp. Taking a final look back toward the river, he tells himself, in the very last sentence of the story, that there will be "plenty of days coming when he could fish the swamp."

Much has been written about the suppressed tension and lingering after-effect of this work, produced in great part by its tautly understated conclusion. Scott Fitzgerald, although he could not quite understand it, thought this one of the most hauntingly beautiful pieces of prose in the English language. Malcolm Cowley was one of the first to discover how the story gained meaning when placed in context with others works, particularly "Now I Lay Me," "A Way You'll Never Be," "In Another Country," and "Chapter VI" of *In Our Time*. But Fitzgerald, Cowley, and other admirers of the story would have been disappointed in their readings had Hemingway kept to his original conclusion.[19] He did, as a matter of fact, stay with it to the extent of advancing it, with minor changes, to what was for him often the publishing stage—namely, typescript.

In both handwritten and typescript form (Items 274 and 275 respectively), the concluding section begins at a point somewhat before that in the published story where Nick hooks the giant trout.[20] It consists mainly of a rambling interior monologue that catalogues those persons, places, and events which have made a strong impression on Hemingway-cum-Nick Adams: Bill Smith, Bill Bird, Hadley Richardson (Helen), Belmonte, Maera, Gertrude Stein, Ezra Pound, James Joyce, Paul Cézanne . . . ; Petoskey,

Horton's Creek, the Black River, Paris, Madrid, Valencia . . . . [21] In discursive fashion, Nick mulls over such matters as fishing, marriage, bull fighting, writing, and painting.

Although Hemingway was to use this method later in "The Snows of Kilimanjaro" and some of the basic material in *A Moveable Feast*, he wisely deleted all of the interior monologue from "Big Two-Hearted River." He submerged the ideas it raised as thoroughly as he had those about the war and Indians. Had they been retained, the story would have emerged as a truncated *Künstlerroman*, a portrait of the artist as a young fisherman—presenting us with a rather self-conscious Nick Adams (the friend of Ezra Pound, Gertrude Stein, and the matador Maera), who is aware of hundreds of tricks in writing invented by James Joyce, and who is himself represented, in dizzying mirror fashion, as the author of "My Old Man" and "Indian Camp." Fortunately, this tricky piece of self-portraiture was, along with everything else in the monologue, excised from the story.

This wholesale act of omission contains several critical implications. Philip Young sees in it a kind of symbolic farewell to youth, to northern Michigan, to marital responsibilities—all of which had to give way to the responsibilities of art. But it is important to note that Hemingway also dropped all considerations of art from the story, except as he may have put them to use in its making. In doing so, he was able to maintain the vital line of his narrative, holding to an existence level of hiking, camping, fishing, eating. Only twice does the published story vary from this basic line of action and thought. The first variance comes near the end of Part I, with the introduction of the "coffee according to Hopkins" episode. And in this instance, when Nick realizes that his mind is "starting to work," he is relieved to discover that he can "choke it," that he can, in other words, suppress any mental activity beyond that needed for existence.

The auctorial suppression revealed by the manuscripts emphasizes the critical fact that "Big Two-Hearted River" is preeminently a story of suppression. Nick Adams is a shadow figure of the author in "choking off" all thoughts about war, art, and civilization as such. Except for the already noted lapse in the Hopkins episode, he holds himself to the simplest of thought processes until the very end of the story, when a concept of tragedy wells up. The singular success of the story is due to the manner in which very primitive matters are accorded very civilized treatment, in terms of emotive restraint and purity of prose. The kind of tension, or balance, Hemingway here achieves accounts for the success of many of his works, most notably perhaps *The Old Man and the Sea*, another account of a solitary fisher. But "Big Two-Hearted River" is subtler, more severely controlled, than any of the other works. Each of its segments consists of a singularly objectified picture that contains, nonetheless, a potentially emotive center. One vital picture follows the other until at the very end some undefined aspect of the human condition hovers in the air, moving well beyond the physical stopping place. In this fictive atmosphere, it is possible to catch some glimmer of a Sisyphean distinction between existence and essence.

To achieve this haunting effect, Hemingway had to do much more than simply eliminate the interior monologue section that threatened to ruin the entire work. He had to re-sight his objective and reconstruct the final scenes. Peculiarly enough, the manuscripts reflect the kind of auctorial enlightenment he went through to attain his end. To see how this happened, it is necessary to examine three particular elements of the conclusion which he prepared in the earliest of the manuscripts (Item 274).

Actually, Hemingway brought this handwritten version of the work to a close twice (see pp. 98 and 99 of Item 274), with a small stutter-step variation thrown in for good measure. Instead of the life-taking incident that informs the conclusion of the published story (the killing of the two trout), Item 274 ends initially on a note of life-preservation similar to that in William Faulkner's "The Bear," where Isaac McCaslin refrains from killing Big Ben. In like manner, Nick Adams decides to set free the giant trout which (in this version of the story) he succeeds in catching, with the declaration that the fish was, after all, "too big to eat."

As though he were not satisfied with this humane gesture, Hemingway added another by tacking on one more page to Item 274. Here, as Nick makes his way back to camp, he finds a stricken rabbit lying "flat out on the trail"—

> There were three ticks on the rabbits head. Two behind one ear and one behind the other. They were gray like the rabbits ear skin, tight with blood, as big as grapes. Nick pulled them off, their heads tiny and hard with moving feet . . . Nick picked up the rabbit, limp, with button eyes, and put it under a sweet fern beside the trail. Its heart was beating as he laid it down. He went on up the trail. *He was holding something in his head.* (p. 99; italics added)

This last page marks a clear advance over the preceding one, where the author had placed first a "30" and two sentences later the words "The End." At these points, Nick simply gets his fishing line caught on a branch and he, like the story, is "stopped" ("30"); and then, after freeing his line, he sets off for camp "his rod out before him" ("The End").

Like a double-exposed photograph, these incidents reflect the predicament of both the author and his character. What Nick and Ernest succeed in freeing is more than a fishing line, for what they eventually hold in their minds is a solution to a problem in artistic representation. Just before and during the fish-freeing and rabbit-saving incidents, Nick has been thinking about Paul Cézanne and certain of his works, including one that depicts "soldiers undressing to swim," and another that shows "the house through the trees." He believes that Cézanne got away from using tricks in his work, that he succeeded in breaking painting down to its essentials, and then proceeded from there. This is why Nick wants "to write the way Cézanne painted."[22] And when he perceives how the French painter would do "this stretch of river," he is filled with a sudden sense of urgency. He wants "to get back to camp and get to work"—presumably on something like the very story in which these matters are being presented. Here again the mirror effect is dizzying, as—

> Nick, seeing how Cézanne would do the stretch of country, stood up. The water was *cold and actual.* He waded across the stream, *moving in the picture.* It was good. He kneeled down in the gravel at the edge of the stream and reached down into the trout sack. The old boy was alive . . . . He slid the trout into the shallow water and watched him move off through the shallows . . . .[23]

This is an intricate passage, mingling actuality with imagination. Nick the author is sketching a picture, and Nick the character is "moving in the picture" as well as the "cold and actual" water, while Hemingway is trying somehow to frame it all off with a proper ending. Of course the irony is that, if Nick (and thus Hemingway) wants to write the way Cézanne painted, he will have to forgo exactly the kind of *trompe l'oeil* trickery employed in the passage quoted above. He will have to get rid of the non-essential interior monologue, including the self-defeating discussion of Joyce's trickery versus Cézanne's integrity. Indeed, he will have to go back to what he had been doing quite simply and naturally earlier in the story—breaking everything down into sharp basic pictures of existence.

This was how Hemingway ultimately solved the problem of ending "Big Two-Hearted River" effectively. Sometime after seeing the original conclusion clearly represented in typescript, he presumably found something more artistically efficacious "in his head" than Nick Adams had. In any event, the published conclusion depends upon a final series of essential "pictures"—man sitting on a log, man eating sandwich, man smoking, man killing two trout, man cleaning trout in cold water, man wading across stream, man climbing an embankment, man walking up path toward camp, and then, most significantly, man taking a last backward glance at where the river narrows and enters the dark swamp. Writing of this kind gains power from its ancient glyphic, pictographic source; it is capable of merging a primitive outer landscape with a sensitive, modern inner one. Done with fine Hemingwaysque detail (down to the milt shucked from the trout), it embodies clarity and mystery at the same time, like Cézanne's painting of the "House of the Hanged Man," which contains no overt sign of either a man or a hanging.

If all this can be characterized as the solution according to Cézanne, it might with some justification also be called a solution according to Henry David Thoreau—that countryman of Hemingway's who, in *Walden* and *A*

Week on the Concord and Merrimack Rivers, proves to be his closest rival
in the literary depiction of the solitary life in the American woods.
Although Hemingway's remarks about Thoreau in *Green Hills of Africa*
indicate no direct line of influence, the two men wrote to the beat of related
drummers. It was, after all, Thoreau who preceded Hemingway with exhor-
tations to "simplify, simplify," to reduce all things to their "lowest common denominator," and to "Say what you have to say, not what you
ought." It was also Thoreau who went before in driving life into a wood-
land corner, there to examine it closely and objectively in order to discover
whether it was "mean" or had sublimity. Hemingway would certainly have
agreed with these pragmatic attitudes and methods, as well as Thoreau's
metaphoric extension of them in such a statement as "Time is but the
stream I go a-fishing in."[24] Moreover, as the manuscripts of "Big Two-
Hearted River" attest, Hemingway was also aware that the artist can control the flow of that stream in his work, and can arrange himself (or a fictional double) just so within the stream, fishing for eternity.

III. "The Short Happy Life"

"The Short Happy Life of Francis Macomber" came out of the same
cluster of experiences that produced *Green Hills of Africa* (1935) and "The
Snows of Kilimanjaro" (1936). Published initially, and somewhat incongru-
ously, in a woman's magazine (*Cosmopolitan*, Sept. 1936), "The Short
Happy Life" was used as the lead story in *The Fifth Column and the First
Forty-nine Stories* in 1938—placed there by an author who listed it first
among his favorites in the short preface he did for this collection. The story
has remained a favorite among anthologists also, with the result that it has
been read and discussed by thousands of college students, and has received
perhaps as much critical attention as any of Hemingway's short narratives.[25] Some of the most important critical questions it has raised deal with
such technical matters as the structure of the work and its shifting point of
view. But within the last decade and a half, a period coinciding with the rise
of the Feminist Movement, most of the questions have concerned such social and moral matters as Robert Wilson's reliability as code hero, Francis
Macomber's conversion from cowardice to courage, and Margot Macomber's motives in her various actions, including the killing of her husband.[26] In certain respects, this critical debate has resembled the line of in-
quiry followed in a court case, with charge and counter-charge, prosecution
and defense, resulting in some rather wilful and even perverse readings of
the story.

If used properly (with due respect for the concept of the intentional fal-
lacy, and with a clear understanding that sub-texts are not to be equated
with *the* text), certain papers in the Hemingway Collection should help answer some of these critical questions, both social and technical, that have

been exacerbated and clouded by partisan furor. The pertinent papers are Item 689, a four-page handwritten beginning of the story; Item 690, a five-page handwritten variation of the previous beginning; Item 692, a one-page handwritten list of sixteen possible titles for the story; and Item 251, a twelve-page typescript entitled "The Art of the Short Story," mentioned previously in connection with "Big Two-Hearted River."

Item 689, the initial beginning, opens with the line "Of course by the third day the old man was gone about her." In narrative tone and method, this fragment represents a peculiar return to those days when a neophyte Hemingway was emulating Sherwood Anderson, particularly in "My Old Man." The first-person narrator of the fragment is an underling who stands in considerable awe of the unnamed white hunter: "I work for him driving cars," he tells us, "so I keep pretty good track of his eyes," and, "he can still spook me with his eyes . . . I can't look at them when he's angry."[27] Through this secondary figure, who is doomed to literary limbo after the second manuscript, we have an opportunity to watch Hemingway's initial attempts to adjust his view and sketch in the necessary elements of his sex triangle. "The husband," we learn, "was one of these Yale old bones men who are so pleasant and such a good fellow and such a fine sportsman that you don't know what it's all about for a long time." The "O. M.," or old man, is "a strange bird," according to the narrator: "You would have to have seen him young to know what it's all about because since cars came in he's got himself covered in a perfect disguise made out of his own body that's put on a belly there and thickened up here and filled his face out so you can't see what it's about."[28]

The wife, named *Dorothy* Macomber in these early versions (her husband is named *Denny*), seemed to be the most difficult of the three major characters to sketch in. It was almost as though there were too much to say about her; and although both manuscripts begin by emphasizing her, supplying a considerable amount of partially conflicting commentary, Hemingway crossed most of this material out, cutting to "the old man" and the way in which he is taken with her beauty. In Item 689, the narrator speaks of her in this manner:

> She was dark and smooth and cool and very expensive looking . . . They're the goddamndest women on earth, really. They only have them in two countries, ours and yours. I suppose they're lovely looking and damned nice if you don't care . . . . And they hunt alone, in pairs, and in packs too . . . She was a fine sample of how good the best of them can look . . . . But they never stop hunting.[29]

In Item 690, a less jumbled and disconnected version, the huntress aspect of the lady is all but eradicated, and her expensive good looks played up:

> She looked like all those pictures of the women who endorse things in the shiny paper magazines. You know, smooth and cool and very expensive. The

kind you can't imagine being mussed or excited or breathing hard or up too early in the morning . . . what we call the backgammon bitches but she was no bitch particularly. No. And the funny thing was she didn't play backgammon either.[30]

Although this entire opening paragraph was eventuallly crossed out, it contained a further concession about Mrs. Macomber in a line that said, "She was a nice enough woman."[31]

The variance in these two early depictions of Margot, *née* Dorothy, Macomber indicate trouble in bringing her into proper narrative focus. Twenty years after the fact, in doing "The Art of the Short Story," Hemingway was much surer about the kind of woman he intended to portray. This unpublished typescript provides us with background information about all three of the major figures in "The Short Happy Life," but most tellingly about the character of Mrs. Macomber:

> This is a simple story in a way, *because the woman, who I knew very well in real life but then invented out of,* to make the woman for this story, is a bitch for the full course and doesn't change. You'll probably never meet the type because you haven't got the money. I haven't either but I get around. Now this woman doesn't change. She has been better, but she will never be better anymore. *I invented her complete with handles* from the worst bitch I knew (then) . . . .

There is more of the same, on the woman, and then on the two men, all of it definite in the mind of the author:

> The woman called Margot Macomber is no good to anybody now except for trouble . . . . The man is a nice jerk. *I knew him very well in real life, so invent him too from everything I know.* So he is just how he really was, *only he is invented.* The White Hunter is my best friend and he does not care what I write as long as it is readable, so I don't invent him at all. I just disguise him for family and business reasons, and to keep him out of trouble with the Game Department.[32]

The reader is, of course, free to accept or reject these hindsight assurances by the author about the nature of his characters. What is more important is that Hemingway, here and elsewhere in this typescript, recognizes the fact that the story makes demands upon the author and shapes his characters, through the invention referred to repeatedly in the italicised phrases above. Until the story shapes up, the characters are still matters of gestation. The manuscript beginnings show this is true not only of the Macombers but also the white hunter—even though Hemingway would later, in characteristically offhand manner, declare that this character was simply his "best friend" disguised "for family and business reasons, and to keep him out of trouble." Yet the "beautiful red-faced Mr. Wilson" who shares his cot with Mrs. Macomber in the finished story is a long imaginative leap away from the fleshy old man with the threatening eyes who is described by the narrator of the two fragments. This early prototype may be more closely aligned with the "Pop" figure of *Green Hills of Africa*, who is based on the real-life Philip Percival. In any event, this old man is "gone about her by the third day," and he "always falls in love with them or thinks he does." Obviously, then, the story demanded a considerably different white hunter, in both attitude and appearance.

If anything, the prototype Francis (Denny) Macomber had to undergo an even more severe adjustment. In the first fragment (Item 689) he is simply presented as a rich Ivy-league type, the necessary appendage of the beautiful wife who is so attractive to the white hunter. All that happens in this instance is that the three of them, described by the self-effacing narrator, engage in conversation around the camp fire:

> Now the wife, Dorothy Macomber, was a lovely looking woman and Macomber was a good looking young fellow and they looked nice sitting there by the fire light in the evening with the O. M., all leaning back in the canvas chairs, she with a gimlet and the two men with whiskeys and sodas and it getting dark and the boys working around their fires.

The only action added to this Abercrombie and Fitch scene is the overhead flight of some flamingoes making a "whicha-whicha-whicha" sound in their "flighting." The old man explains that they are on their way to a nearby lake, where they may be seen "in the daytime." The fragment breaks off just after Mrs. Macomber responds to this information, saying, "It's wonderful. . . . Aren't you glad we came, Denny?"

These flamingoes fly off and are never heard of again. The second manuscript makes no mention of them, nor does it use this campfire scene. It establishes the camp and then moves off to hunting territory. There, through a series of actions, it fills out the character of Macomber considerably. In fact, this version focuses fully on him, presenting him as an intriguing, perhaps even dominating figure, and above all an extraordinarily good shot. As the narrator relates matters:

> . . . the old man took them out to Mutu-umbu to see if they could learn to shoot a little first. We camped there in the big trees and took them up the valley the next morning. This fellow Macomber, the husband, was a good shot. He made a nice shot on a wildebeeste. Then he made a hell of a good shot on quite a good Grant.

When the old man wants to see more of his clients' shooting ability, the party drives off to where there is a herd of "Tommys" (Thomson's East Africa gazelle), and Macomber is set up for a very difficult piece of hunting:

> So Macomber gets out and sits down and we drive away about four hundred yards and the Tommys move off too. What he has now is a hell of a shot, the wind is blowing a big breeze and the light has started to get that heat haze. It was a long shot and a bad one to make. I wouldn't have tried it. But we saw him sitting there, comfortable looking, well back on his heels, using the sling

to steady himself in the wind and saw the rifle spit and whack the Tommy was down and the rest of them bounding off . . . . We drove over and he came walking up.

The manuscript here becomes repetitively insistent about Macomber's ability. The old man questions him about what windage adjustment he had made and the spot he had aimed for; after examining the dead animal he declares, "Well, you *can* shoot . . . That was a damned fine shot," and a bit later repeats, "You can shoot." But Macomber's reaction to this accolade from the master is noteworthy. As the narrator observes, "Macomber didn't seem very pleased and he didn't seem very happy."

Two paragraphs later the fragment stops. In the first of these it is established that Mrs. Macomber is an unexceptional shot: "The woman could shoot just like any woman," the chauvinist narrator declares—"She could hit them fine and miss them just as well and didn't know why she did either." Again, however, he returns to the husband, stating, " . . . this fellow Macomber was a rifle shot. But there was something funny about him." The something funny is emphasized in the last paragraph, which describes the party sitting around in camp drinking: the old man and Dorothy Macomber begin to "feel good," but as the very last lines inform us, "Macomber was serious as hell and wanted to talk about shock, and penetration and all the rest of it."

What kind of story would "The Short Happy Life," with this or some other title, have turned into had Hemingway continued with this manuscript beginning? Would it have ended with Mrs. Macomber killing her husband, or with her husband, that strangely intense and expert shot, killing her or the white hunter, or both? Was Hemingway preparing for a zany duel between white hunter and husband, to be brought on by the wife's sexual transgression? Unless other papers are discovered, we will never know. Perhaps the author was already preparing to contrast Macomber's ability to shoot with his inability to act courageously in hunting dangerous game. And perhaps the ending of the story as we know it is foreshadowed in the line about Mrs. Macomber's ability with a gun—"She could hit them fine and miss them just as well and didn't know why she did either."

We do know Hemingway solved the narrative problems implicit in the two manuscript beginnings. The first thing he did was to get rid of the awkward first-person narrator. In doing so, he shifted to an omniscient point of view, but with a special built-in hall of mirrors feature that allowed him to round out, and at the same time deepen, the major characters. "The Short Happy Life," along with "The Snows of Kilimanjaro," stands as one of Hemingway's most technically intricate and subtle works, mainly because of the various angles of vision and perception it provides. Although the story operates on a point-counterpoint principle, we perceive fear, cowardice, humiliation, the need to learn, and finally the exhilaration of courage mainly through the sensibilities of Francis Macomber. The values of rich clients, the vicious games that they play, the American battle of the sexes, the management of hunting activities, the sexual attractiveness of Margot Macomber, the need for some kind of code of personal and professional behavior, and the reactions of Margot after the shooting of her husband—all of these things are made known to us from Robert Wilson's angle of perception.

Most of the story, in fact, is told from these alternating male points of view. Only a few times does Hemingway resort to other viewpoints. Twice he makes important use of Margot as viewer and assessor, once near the beginning of the story and once toward the end. In both instances we see the two men through her eyes:

> She looked at both these men as though she had never seen them before.
>
> One, Wilson . . . , she knew she had never truly seen before. He was about middle height with sandy hair, a stubby mustache, a very red face and extremely cold blue eyes with faint white wrinkles at the corners that grooved merrily when he smiled. He smiled at her now and she looked away from his face at the way his shoulders sloped in the loose tunic he wore with the four big cartridges held in loops . . . .

This is a fairly frank appraisal of masculine, perhaps even priapic, attractiveness, reminding the reader of Liz Coates' appraisal of Jim Gilmore in "Up In Michigan." Here Francis Macomber suffers by contrast, for though he is a handsome young man (of thirty-five), he has "just shown himself, very publicly, to be a coward." In the second instance, however, Margot sees the two men in a different relationship, as comrades in arms:

> From the far corner of the [car] seat Margot Macomber looked at the two of them. There was no change in Wilson. She saw Wilson as she had seen him the day before when she had first realized what his great talent was. But she saw the change in Francis now.

It may be true that Hemingway was psychically incapable of seeing more of any story from a female point of view: none of his works show the hermaphroditic sensibilities that produced Emma Bovary, Anna Karenina, and the insatiable Molly Bloom. But there are two good reasons for holding mainly to the male angles of vision in "The Short Happy Life": the first of these is technical, and the second, as we shall see, is thematic.

Technically, the plot demands that the reader not know for certain what goes through Margot Macomber's mind when she shoots her husband. To have placed emphasis on her thought processes throughout the narrative and then to have avoided her thoughts and feelings at the crucial point, would have severely damaged the artistic integrity of the story. As it was, Hemingway had to work very carefully at this vital juncture in his narrative, resorting to auctorial reportage, and stating that "Mrs. Macomber, in the car, *had shot at the buffalo as it seemed about to gore Macomber,* and had hit her husband about two inches up and a little to one side of the base of his skull." The italicized section of the passage (italics added) is quoted in part by Warren Beck in his article entitled "The Shorter Happy Life of Mrs. Macomber." He offers the words "shot at the buffalo" as proof of the lady's innocence, stating that although Hemingway was "a highly implicative artist," he was not "notably given to double talk."[33] Had he had access to "The Art of the Short Story," Beck might have been less sure about his statement, for in that piece Hemingway concludes his remarks about "The Short Happy Life" in a contradictory manner:

> That about handles that story. Any questions? No, I don't know whether she shot him on purpose any more than you do. I could find out if I asked myself because I invented it and I could go right on inventing. But you have to know where to stop. That is what makes a short story. Makes it short at least. The only hint I could give you is that it is my belief that the incidence of husbands shot accidentally by wives who are bitches and really work at it is very low. Should we continue?

In between the wise-guy comments, we catch sight of the integrity that separates the artist from the man. It is the artist in Hemingway that says, "I don't know whether she shot him on purpose any more than you do." And it is the artist who must give Mrs. Macomber her due, allowing for psychological ambiguity, and keeping the fictional case moot—in between involuntary manslaughter and second-degree murder (perpetrated with a 6.5 *Mannlicher,* which Mark Spilka has noted means "manly" in German and suggests man-licker, or -defeater, in English).[34]

As we can see from observation of the wavering manuscript beginnings, with their indefinite stereotype figures, Hemingway finally constructed his characters as the plot demanded. Each of the three major figures is flawed in personality. Macomber has been a spoiled young rich man, a cowardly cuckold, and an amoral materialist who knows something about motor cars and "court games" but very little about men and women. Mrs. Macomber is represented as being equally amoral and materialistic—a woman who has used her beauty as a social and economic stay, and her sexual transgressions, both past and present, as an assertive club. Robert Wilson is a hunting guide who is himself guided by the tawdry standards of his pre-jet-set clients in all things except hunting, and who bends the rules of his profession as he sees fit. It should be noted, however, that Wilson does try to live up to his own personal code, even if he is not "a bloody plaster saint." Moreover, he possesses what for Hemingway and the old Stoic philosophers is the *sine qua non* of all human virtues—courage.

In Wilson's understanding of male courage we find the thematic, and thus structural, reason for Hemingway's holding mainly to the contrapuntal viewpoints of the two men in this story. Wilson, we learn, has "seen men

come of age before and it always moved him." It moves him to view
Macomber's transformation in this perceptive and sympathetic fashion:

> Beggar had probably been afraid all his life. Don't know what started it. But
> over now. Hadn't had time to be afraid of the [buffalo]. That and being an-
> gry too. Motor car too. Motor cars made it familiar . . . More of a change
> than any loss of virginity. Fear gone like an operation. Something else grew in
> its place. Main thing a man had . . . . [35]

This passage emphasizes the fact that, thematically, "The Short Happy
Life" is above all a compressed *Bildungsroman,* or more precisely,
Erziehungsroman, which might very well have been labelled "The Educa-
tion of Francis Macomber."

Structurally, the story depends upon a sometimes obscured catechism of
direct and indirect questions and answers. In fact, the beginning of the story
that Hemingway finally devised centers on the seemingly unimportant question of what one should drink at lunch on an African safari. It begins in the
middle of things, with Macomber, already the odd man out, asking, "Will
you have lime juice or lemon squash? Robert Wilson and Margot Macomber brush aside the implicit suggestion of a soft drink, declaring the necessity of something alcoholic under the circumstances. Macomber capitulates in
his response: "I suppose it's the thing to do . . . . Tell him to make it three
gimlets." [36]

Just a partial list of these questions shows how they run the gamut from
the most trivial customs to the most vital aspects of morality, ethics, and
law:

> *How much should the "beaters" be tipped after a hunt?*
> *Should one wear one's hat at noon, "even under the canvas"?*
> *May a Swahili servant stare at a hunting client, even a cowardly one?*
> *Is it permissible to punish such a servant by whipping him?*
> *Should a white hunter tell tales about a client?*
> *Should the client ask that information about him be suppressed?*
> *How should the hunter behave afterward in the company of a client who*
> *makes such a request?*
> *How should the client react after he realizes how cowardly he has been?*
> *Should a wife shoot at a charging buffalo when there is a good chance she will*
> *kill her husband in the process?*

There are many more such questions imbedded in the story—about whether
it is legal to hunt from moving vehicles, and, of course, what must be done
after wounding a lion. Some of these pertain directly to Margot Macomber,
like that asked by Robert Wilson: *"How should a woman act when she discovers her husband is a bloody coward?"* And, indeed, the ending of the
story—built on the moot point of whether she shot her husband purposely
or accidentally—asks how a wife should behave after she has shot her husband.

As the story is constructed, however, Robert Wilson functions as the catechist and Francis Macomber as the principal catechumen. The main lesson to be learned is not how to hunt lions or buffalo, but how to face up to life. And in terms of the way in which Hemingway built this story, finishing off a wounded lion or standing up to a charging buffalo is no more important than learning how to face up to one's wife.

Along with its companion piece, "The Snows of Kilimanjaro," this story of Mr. and Mrs. Macomber helps expand the series of short narratives Hemingway had already done about the battle of the sexes—including "The Doctor and the Doctor's Wife," "Mr. and Mrs. Elliot," "Cat in the Rain," "Out of Season," "Cross-Country Snow," "Hills Like White Elephants," "A Canary for One," "The Sea Change," and "Homage to Switzerland." Anyone who has read these works closely knows that Hemingway represented male and female characters with varying degrees of sympathy. In some, the female character is fine and understanding, while the male is insensitive and cloddish (as in "Cat in the Rain" and "Hills Like White Elephants"); in others, the female is insensitive and cruel, while the male is weak and maltreated (as in "The Doctor and the Doctor's Wife" and "Mr. and Mrs. Elliot").

What Hemingway had to do in "The Short Happy Life" was to fuse the matter of matrimonial struggle with the hunt and the temporary emergence of a self-respecting man. His task is made apparent by a note he wrote to himself on a sheet of paper (Item 692), on which he also listed sixteen possible titles for this story. The note simply says:

> To look up
> Man
> Marriage
> Fear
> Courage.

The titles reinforce the note. Most of them refer directly or indirectly to marriage; others intertwine marriage and hunting; and the remainder (like "The New Man" and the title eventually selected, with one important modification) point toward Macomber's transformation:

> A Marriage Has Been Arranged
> The Coming Man
> The New Man
> The Short Life of Francis Macomber [sic]
> The End of the Marriage
> Marriage Is a Dangerous Game
> The More Dangerous Game
> A Marriage Has Been Terminated
> The Ruling Classes

The Fear of Courage
Brief Mastery
The Master Passion

The Cult of Violence
The Struggle for Power [in margin]

Marriage is a Bond
Through Darkest Marriage [back of photocopy][37]

Hemingway was as careful and precise in the selection of titles as he was in the actual writing and revision of his works. At times he used working titles during the early stages of composition (*The World's Room* and *Nights and Forever* were so used for *A Farewell to Arms*), but most often it was Hemingway's practice to make up lists of potential titles during the revision stage of composition, or, as he informed George Plimpton, after a work was actually finished.[38] With "The Short Happy Life" it would appear that he followed his usual practice. There were no working titles attached to the early manuscripts; and the thematic inclusiveness of the sixteen titles in Item 692 indicates that the author had the story well in mind, either finished or nearly so, by the time he made up the list.

In this instance, the titles are somewhat different from others devised by Hemingway, who tended toward literary allusion and resonance, or the indication of climatic, topographic, or geographic features (as with *For Whom the Bell Tolls*, "Cross-Country Snow," "Hills Like White Elephants," and "The Snows of Kilimanjaro," which combines two of these features). Only one of the titles listed above makes even indirect reference to a geographic element, with the reworking of the common phrase "through darkest Africa" into "Through Darkest Marriage." And only one has literary reference. With "The More Dangerous Game" Hemingway was referring to a cheap thriller of his day, Richard Connell's "The Most Dangerous Game," published in 1924. This, too, is a hunting story, but with an implausible plot, unbelievable characters (two big-game hunters who try to kill each other), and what Hemingway would call a "wow ending."

It was Hemingway the self-editor who rejected "The More Dangerous Game," with its oblique reference to Connell's soggy story, and with its harsh suggestion that women are more dangerous than wounded lions or buffalo. It was Hemingway the artist who selected "The Short Life of Francis Macomber" and added the vital attributive adjective "Happy" to it, applying the revised title as thematic indicator and capstone. Years later, in "The Art of the Short Story," Hemingway the man would express considerable satisfaction with both his titular selection and narrative accomplishment. "Now there is another story called The Short Happy Life of Francis Macomber," he begins in that offhand manner he affects throughout most of this piece: "Jack, I get a bang even yet from just writing the titles. That's why you write, no matter what they tell you."

And that, as the papers indicate, is why you *rewrite* also, fusing the talents of the writer and the self-editor to produce literary works that we can all get a "bang" out of. The manuscripts examined here show that Hemingway was capable of cold editorial excision—in cutting away the first half of "Indian Camp," and in removing the bulge of reminiscence and artistic commentary that threatened the vital flow of "Big Two-Hearted River." He had the ability to reject stock situations and stereotyped characters, to begin again, and again if necessary, to discover where he was really headed with a story like "The Short Happy Life." Through such examples we learn much about Hemingway's process of composition—how he omitted unnecessary information; how he discovered better points of view and deeper points of interest; and how, in some instances, he shed personal prejudices or attitudes to produce works of universal appeal.

Of course, the papers do not tell us everything. We have no manuscript, for example, that tells how Hemingway reworked the plot of "The Short Happy Life"—by employing a central flashback to Macomber's act of cowardice, so that he was able to construct an inductive mystery, beginning with the "lemon squash" and "gimlets" dialogue, which nicely sets the tone for the entire catechism of questions and answers that follows. Nor do we have a variant manuscript that tells when, or *why*, Hemingway decided to inject into the story that tour de force segment in which he perceives things from the viewpoint of the hunted lion.[39]

Besides the lessons briefly reviewed here, however, there are many others to be learned from Hemingway's handling of beginnings and endings as reflected in the manuscripts. It is the job of criticism to determine, in each instance, what is known and what is unknown, and perhaps unknowable, since much of creation remains hidden from the eye, sometimes even the eye of the creator. Beyond this, all the critic can do, even with privileged peeks behind the curtain, is to prepare a set of clumsy and partial blueprints that may, despite their inadequacies, reveal the problems and beauties of the finished structures, and provide all readers with a better basis of analysis and appreciation than they might otherwise have.

NOTES

1 See Philip Young and Charles W. Mann, "Fitzgerald's *Sun Also Rises:* Notes and Comment," *Fitzgerald/Hemingway Annual 1970* (Washington, D. C.: NCR Microcard Editions, 1970), pp. 1-9.

2 Bernard Oldsey, *Hemingway's Hidden Craft: The Writing of "A Farewell to Arms"* (University Park, Pa.: Pennsylvania State Univ. Press, 1979), pp. 74-5.

3 Ibid., pp. 71-91, 100-10.

4 Ibid., pp. 57-68.

5 All of the publication information about Hemingway's works used in this study is taken from Audre Hanneman's *Ernest Hemingway: A Comprehensive Bibliography* (Princeton, N. J.: Princeton Univ. Press, 1967); see p. 8 in this instance.

6 Julian Smith, "Hemingway and the Thing Left Out," as reprinted in *Ernest Hemingway: Five Decades of Criticism,* ed. Linda W. Wagner (East Lansing, Mich.: Michigan State Univ. Press, 1974), p. 189.

7 Ibid., p. 199.

8 " 'Big World Out There': The Nick Adams Stories," in *The Short Stories of Ernest Hemingway: Critical Essays,* ed. Jackson J. Benson (Durham, N. C.: Duke Univ. Press, 1975), p. 32. In this essay, written originally to act as an introduction to *The Nick Adams Stories,* Young led the way in making manuscript information count for something in the critical reconsideration of Hemingway stories.

9 Ibid.

10 See Item 493 in the Hemingway Collection.

11 Item 493, italics added. In the line preceding the first end mark of "30," a mark which was then crossed out, Hemingway had written the word *shell*; afterward he wrote over the *s*, making it a *c*, and then placing a dot over the *e*, changed the word *shell* to *chill*.

12 In Item 493 the last sentence appears to have been added as an afterthought, and then built up with modifying phrases.

13 *Stephen Crane: An Omnibus*, ed. R. W. Stallman (N. Y.: Knopf, 1952), p. 369.

14 Although the catalogue of the Hemingway Collection identifies this item (251) as having a full title in note form of "The Art of the Short Story and Nine Stories to Prove It," the only title given on the typescript itself is "The Art of the Short Story." Dated from La Consula, Churriana; Malaga, Spain—June, 1959, it appears to have been written as a preface for a forthcoming collection of Hemingway's stories, but which one is not clear.

[After hearing this article read, Mr. Charles Scribner, Jr. informed the author that "The Art of the Short Story" was prepared as an introduction for *The Snows of Kilimanjaro and Other Stories* (N. Y.: Scribner's, 1961). "When we rejected it," Mr. Scribner said, "that was the sorest I can ever remember Hemingway being with me. He was really mad. But luckily Mary agreed with me that it wasn't suitable."]

15 Italics added.

16 Here, as in a number of his manuscripts, Hemingway reveals his tendency to begin stories with the names of actual persons (like *Scott Fitzgerald*, a name that lasted all the way into the first publication of "The Snows of Kilimanjaro," and *Ag*—for Agnes von Kurowsky, that did the same in "A Very Short Story").

17 Carlos Baker, following in the path of Malcolm Cowley's remarks in *The Portable Hemingway,* states this critical perçu succinctly and well: "In some special way, the destroyed town of Seney and the scorched earth around it carry the hint of war—the area of destruction Nick must pass through in order to reach the high rolling pine plain where the excorcism is to take place." See Baker's *Hemingway: The Writer as Artist*, 3rd ed. (Princeton: Princeton Univ. Press, 1963), p. 127.

18 See Carl Ficken's close analysis of "Point of View in the Nick Adams Stories," as reprinted in *The Short Stories of Ernest Hemingway,*" ed. Benson (op. cit), pp. 106-7.

19 The standard traumatic-therapeutic reading is Philip Young's—in *Ernest Hemingway: A Reconsideration* (University Park, Pa: Pennsylvania State University Press, 1966), pp. 43-48. Needless to stress, there could have been no such reading had Hemingway held to his earlier line.

20 These are represented, with certain changes made, in the selection entitled "On Writing," in *The Nick Adams Stories* (N.Y.: Scribners's, 1972).

21 There are some forty specific places and persons that enter into this monologue section. Theodore Dreiser and Sherwood Anderson are mentioned among the other writers, like Joyce, Pound, and Stein.

22 See Raymond S. Nelson, *Hemingway: Expressionist Artist* (Ames, Iowa: Iowa State Univ. Press, 1979). Nelson uses some of this material, taken from an account by Carlos Baker, but seems not to have availed himself of the pertinent Hemingway papers or the piece "On Writing" in *The Nick Adams Stories*.

23 See Item 274, pp. 96-7; italics added.

24 These lines from Thoreau are to be found in the widely used *Walden and Civil Disobedience*, ed. Sherman Paul (Boston: Houghton Mifflin, 1960), pp. 62, 223, 68, respectively.
It is worth noting that, during this period of composing his African works, Hemingway did have Thoreau on his mind. In an early version of "The Snows of Kilimanjaro" he gave his protagonist the name of "Henry Walden."

25 With notes, articles, and commentaries in books, the critical bibliography on "The Short Happy Life" would run well over fifty items. Among the most important of these items are the following: Ronald S. Crane, "Ernest Hemingway: 'The Short Happy Life of Francis Macomber,' " in *The Idea of the Humanities and Other Essays Critical and Historical,* Vol. 2 (Chicago: Univ. of Chicago Press, 1967), 315-26. James G. Watson, " 'A Sound Basis of Union': Structural and Thematic Balance in 'The Short Happy Life of Francis Macomber,' " *Fitzgerald/Hemingway Annual*, 1974, pp. 215-28. Warren Beck, "The Shorter Happy Life of Mrs. Macomber," *Modern Fiction Studies*, 21 (Autumn 1975), 363-76, with an afterword in which Beck discusses the original publication of his essay and the comments made on it by Mark Spilka. Mark Spilka, "The Necessary Stylist: A New Critical Revision," *Modern Fiction Studies*, 6 (Winter 1960-61), 283-97; and "Warren Beck Revisited," *Modern Fiction Studies*, 22 (Summer 1976), 245-55.

26 In addition to the works by Beck and Spilka mentioned above, see Virgil Hutton, "The Short Happy Life of Macomber," reprinted in *The Short Stories of Ernest Hemingway: Critical Essays*, ed. Jackson J. Benson, op. cit., pp. 239-50. Robert B. Holland, "Macomber and the Critics," *Studies in Short Fiction*, 5 (Winter 1968), 171-78. John S. Hill, "Robert Wilson: Hemingway's Judge in Macomber," *University Review*, 35 (Winter 1968), 129-32. Anne Greco, "Margot Macomber: 'Bitch Goddess' Exonerated," *Fitzgerald/Hemingway Annual*, 1972.

27 It is difficult to speculate about the age or the background of this narrator. Al-

though his speech pattern is American, there is a hint later that he might be British.

28 This out-of-shape character, who has become overly dependent upon motor vehicles, seems quite some imaginative distance away from Robert Wilson.

29 Here the narrator speaks of "two countries, ours and yours." Is he referring to the U.S. and Great Britain, or the U.S. and some other country? Nothing in the manuscript makes this clear. The phrase could be an ironic ploy, meaning *any* other country, and "yours."

30 Interjected lines and cross-outs make this passage from Item 690 and the previous one quoted from Item 689 somewhat difficult to represent; but as they are quoted here, these passages contain all but the most minor elements, and in as close to manuscript order as is editorially possible.

31 The narrator is less interested in Mrs. Macomber than is the O. M., but the narrator shows early signs of Hemingway's attempt to represent the female character of his story objectively.

32 Italics added. (Hemingway continued with his insistence on inventing character: "This information is what you call the background of a story. You throw it all away and invent from what you know.")

33 *Modern Fiction Studies*, 21 (Autumn 1975), 375.

34 "Warren Beck Revisited," *Modern Fiction Studies*, 22 (Summer 1976), 253.

35 Robert Wilson here shows a concern and an understanding that the Wilson haters do not seem to take into consideration. Virgil Hutton (see note 26 of this study) seems to be the most vindictive, almost critically perverse, of the anti-Wilson partisans. He reads everything in the story as an indication of how hateful a bully Wilson is, how hypocritical a guide and judge. In fact, he tries to show how Hemingway himself undercut Wilson through having him advance the Shakespearian line (about owing God "one life," etc.) in ignorance of its real meaning. Anyone who knows Hemingway's life and work knows he doted on this saying, using it as a clue to courage for men going off to war, in the anthology he edited during World War II, entitled *Men At War*.

36 In a manuscript scheduled for journal publication this coming spring, Bert Bender (in "Margot Macomber's Gimlet") analyzes this opening scene and the symbolic meaning of this drink in an ingenious and meaningful way.

37 It is difficult to know whether this is one sheet, front and back, or just one page in photo-reproduction. [The author is grateful to Leger Brosnahan, who provided the following information after hearing this article read: "A forthcoming study of the carbon copy used in the setting of the collected edition of the story, shows that the story went untitled until the completion of the final typed copy . . ."]

In addition, it should be noted that only one of the ten tentative titles listed by John M. Howell and Charles Lawler in *Proof*, 2 (1972), 217-18, appears in Item 692. Those represented by Howell and Lawler run as follows: Than a Dead Lion, The Manner of the Accident, Fear's End, The Short Happy Life of Francis Macomber (with the "Happy" in place), The Tragic Safari, The Lion's Portion, Mr. and Mrs. Macomber, The Macombers, The Macomber Safari, and The Safari of Francis Macomber (with full allusion to the saint, martyrdom, as well as the birds and the beasts).

Also in *A Life Story* (p. 284), Baker states that Hemingway "completed a story, tentatively called 'The Happy Ending,'" still another designation.

38 See pp. 14-16 in *Hemingway's Hidden Craft*. Hemingway told Plimpton, in their *Paris Review* interview that he made "a list of titles after" finishing a story or book—"sometimes as many as a hundred." There is good evidence, however, that he often started the titling process during revision periods, and sometimes even earlier.

39 This may very well have been a narrative mistake, and one not typical of Hemingway, who elsewhere shows the ability to cut unnecessary stuff. In "The Art of the Short Story," Hemingway speaks defensively about inclusion of this material: "That's all there is to that story except maybe the lion when he is hit and I am thinking inside of him really, not faked. I can think inside of a lion, really. It's hard to believe and it is perfectly okay with me if you don't believe it. Perfectly." He then goes on to discuss some unnamed writer who used the same method of narrating from an animal point of view, "making only one mistake." He then adds, somewhat ruefully, "Making any mistake kills you. This mistake killed him and quite soon everything he wrote was a mistake." Obviously all this still weighed on Hemingway's mind, twenty years after the story was published.

Howell and Lawler (see note 37) make a good point about the function of the lion in respect to Macomber's change from the status of a cowardly, bolting "rabbit" to a dying but dignified lion. Without solving the problem of potential ambiguity and irony, they point to two of the tentative titles as being meaningful in this respect—"The Lion's Portion," as in the expression "the lion's share"; and "Than a Dead Lion," an allusion to Ecclesiastes (9: 4) and the idea that "a living dog is better than a dead lion."

"PROUD AND FRIENDLY AND GENTLY": WOMEN IN HEMINGWAY'S EARLY FICTION

Linda W. Wagner

When F. Scott Fitzgerald commented to Hemingway that Catherine Barkley in *A Farewell to Arms* is less successful than some of the women from his early short stories, he showed again his acute literary judgment. As Fitzgerald phrases it, "in the stories you were really listening to women—here you're only listening to yourself."[1] Whatever the reason for the distancing that was to mar Hemingway's portrayal of women characters from 1929 on (except for Pilar, Maria, and Marie Morgan), there is little question that Hemingway was at his most sympathetic and skillful in drawing the female leads of the short stories of *In Our Time* and *Men Without Women* and of *The Sun Also Rises*. His manuscripts show that Hemingway was also comfortable with those portrayals, seldom making changes—except very minor ones—between what appears to be first draft and final versions.

One of the most striking characteristics of Hemingway's women in his early fiction is their resemblance to the later, mature Hemingway hero. It is primarily Brett Ashley's similarity to Jake Barnes that marks her as an aficionado of life (her phrase describing Count Mippipopolous as "one of us"[2] indicates that she knows the parallels, and bases her judgments of people on criteria similar to those Jake uses). But in fact, in Hemingway's earlier stories—"Up in Michigan," "Indian Camp," "The End of Something," "The Three-Day Blow," and "Cross-Country Snow"—the women have already reached that plateau of semi-stoic self awareness which Hemingway's men have, usually, yet to attain.

When Marjorie understands her rejection in "The End of Something," she behaves so admirably that Nick feels the impact of his loss doubly, and continues to mourn it throughout "The Three-Day Blow." " 'I'm taking the boat,' " she called to him as she moved away, out of reach of both touch and sound. What the expected female behavior was is indicated a few lines later as Bill appears on the scene:

"Did she go all right?" Bill said.

"Yes," Nick said, lying, his face on the blanket.

"Have a scene?"

"No, there wasn't any scene."

"How do you feel?"

"Oh, go away, Bill! Go away for a while."[3]

If Hemingway/Nick were to choose at that moment, he would surely prefer Marjorie's pride and grace to Bill's insensitive smirking.

"The End of Something" is one of the earliest of Hemingway's well-made, well-imaged stories. In these, much characterization is accomplished through the attribution of the insightful perception. Marjorie, here, sees the old mill as both an emblem of their relationship ("There's our old ruin, Nick") and something magical ("It seems more like a castle"). In response to each suggestion, "Nick said nothing." An early version of the dialogue gives us Nick as a sharp-tongued anti-romantic:

"What's that ruin, Nick?"
"It's Stroud's old mill."
"It looks like a castle."
"Not much."[4]

An inability to see clearly, perceptively, is Robert Cohn's flaw by the time of *The Sun Also Rises*; finding these early male protagonists—Nick, Bill, Harold Krebs—marked by the same insensitivity provides interesting parallels. Truly stories of male initiation, the short stories of *In Our Time* and *Men Without Women* tend to give us male characters who *need* that initiation. They learn from Hemingway's women. Or, tragically, they fail to learn.

In "Hills Like White Elephants" Hemingway employs exactly the same technique. Although the characters are introduced with apparent objectivity as "the American and the girl with him," Hemingway's sympathy is clearly with the girl—*Jig*, in the published story; *Hadley*, in the manuscript. The girl is perceptive, tranquil, troubled but not vindictive; despite all her conflicts and sorrows over the impending abortion, she behaves with "grace under pressure." Again, Hemingway conveys her superior vision through the title image:

The girl was looking off at the line of hills.
They were white in the sun and the country was brown and dry.
"They look like white elephants," she said.
"I've never seen one," the man drank his beer.
"No, you wouldn't have."

His literalness, his inability to respond to play are negative qualities in themselves, but the dialogue continues to give him even more abrasive responses:

"I might have," the man said. "Just because you say I wouldn't have doesn't prove anything."
The girl looked at the bead curtain. "They've painted something on it . . . ."[5]

She deflects the argument, although the rest of the story is a marvel of dialogue between the rational male ("It's perfectly simple . . . . It's really not anything. It's just to let the air in . . . . It's really an awfully simple opera-

tion . . . . it's perfectly simple . . . . it's the best thing to do . . . . It's really
not an operation at all . . . . it's all perfectly natural") and the distraught
woman, who finally—three pages of his quarrelsome reassurance
later—manages to ask, with only a little loss of control,

> "Would you do something for me now?"
> "I'd do anything for you."
> "Would you please please please please please please please stop talking?"

"I'll scream" the girl continues as he begins the repetitive reassurances, and
one can imagine the months of days and nights already given to this one-
sided, cliched discussion. In lines deleted from the final version, Hemingway has the American go to the bar and think, with dismay,

> There must be some place you could touch where people were calm and rea-
> sonable.[6]

In the revision of the early manuscript, Hemingway has carefully given
the perception of the title image to the woman. In the earlier and finally incomplete version, the man and the woman shared the perception, but the
image served no purpose.[7] The story originally became trapped in the tavern
and on the train, with no mention of anything significant between the characters. We never know it is an abortion story, and Hemingway abandons it,
unfinished. The early version, as the character's name indicates, was Hadley's story; the finished version carries an epigraph line, "For Pauline—well, well, well."[8] Whatever else had happened to him in the 1920's,
Hemingway had found a structure that would make "Hills Like White Elephants" work as a story of a strong, and sympathetic, female character.

One might surmise that "Cat in the Rain" is a continuation of the same
story, and that the young wife's frustration with her lonely and ultimately
unsettled, infertile existence stems from another impending abortion. The
changes that Hemingway makes in the manuscript are all directed toward
making George unsympathetic, setting him in contrast to the gracious hotel
keeper who understands the woman's need to care for and to be cared for.
In her climactic closing speech, when she longs for stability and a home,
Hemingway gives us the clue to her unhappiness:

> "I'd like to pull my hair back tight and smooth and make a big knot and
> wear a Spanish comb and have on a Yteb gown and a cat to sit in my lap and
> purr in front of the fire while I waited for someone to come home."
> "You're a swell mixture," George said.
> "I want a table set with my own silver and candles lit—and I don't want to
> know what's going to happen."[9]

The final version has, of course, deleted that last sentence (as well as rearranged the lines for rhythmic impact and thematic emphasis) but the poig-
nance remains. George, hiding in his book, listening only in order to rest his
eyes, parallels the reasonable American of "Hills Like White Elephants"

and the adolescently selfish Nick and Bill of "The Three-Day Blow" and "The End of Something."

It can certainly be said that fascination with women characters, if not the characters themselves, dominates *In Our Time*. The original epigraph points to this fascination:

A Girl in Chicago: Tell us about the French women, Hank. What are they like?

Bill Smith: How old are the French women, Hank?[10]

Although the interspersed vignettes might suggest more externally oriented themes of war and bullfighting, of the stories included in the collection, only five or six have a focus other than a woman character or a relationship. And even within the vignettes, a character's humanity is gauged by his or her sympathy toward the life processes—birth as well as death.

It seems very clear that, at this point in his career, Hemingway was as interested in women characters as he was in men—perhaps more interested. As he had written in 1956,

I have always considered that it was easy to be a man compared to being a woman who lives by as rigid standards as men live by. No one of us lives by as rigid standards nor has as good ethics as we planned but an attempt is made.[11]

And he continued in his 1959 "The Art of the Short Story," "It is hardest to do about women and you must not worry when they say there are no such women as those you wrote about. That only means your women aren't like their women."[12] The defensive tone in Hemingway's comments is probably explained by the negative criticism many of his woman characters—if noticed at all—had received. Not until Alan Holder's brief 1963 essay, "The Other Hemingway," had much attention been paid to his mastery of characterization of women.[13]

The fictionalization of Brett Ashley in *The Sun Also Rises* had in fact created many problems for Hemingway. Rather than being acclaimed as a warm, believable, brave woman, Brett was frequently maligned as unnatural, bold, nymphomaniacal.[14] Hemingway had never intended Brett to be an affront; she was to have gained readers' sympathy and admiration, and thereby buttressed the positive elements of Jake Barnes' persona. After such misreading, Hemingway may have been hesitant to trust his readers with what he thought were interesting women. Part of the submissiveness and languor of Catherine Barkley may have stemmed from what he thought was lack of appreciation of Brett's "nobility."

Also, had *The Sun Also Rises* been published as Hemingway had written it, much of the misreading of Brett would probably not have occurred. His deletion of the first chapter and part of the second—much material which explained and explored Brett as bereaved and betrayed war victim—left readers too little direction. Even though Fitzgerald's suggestion to cut this opening was made as a friendly gesture (to scuttle the random writing that plagued Hemingway at his most self-conscious), it has caused readers problems.[15]

The first chapter of the book—cut only after it was in galley proofs—was a positive presentation of Brett—broke, afraid of being alone. "This is a novel about a lady. Her name is Lady Ashley and when the story begins she is living in Paris and it is Spring. That should be a good setting for a romantic but highly moral story."[16] Hemingway then recounts Brett's grace, her style, her ability to weather all kinds of bad experiences: "Brett was a very happy person." We are treated to a description of her first husband's tying her up in her kitchen, to the financial uncertainty of her life. The first chapter closes with the foreshadowing for what was to be an *a*typical situation for Brett: "Brett was left alone in Paris. She had never been very good at being alone."

The irony of the novel (set in the spring, among people heading for a "fiesta" as the British title for the book emphasizes) echoes the strange experience of everyone's going on vacation, and Brett alone. What Hemingway was portraying was hardly a normal life for expatriates.

Chapter II, much of which was also omitted, focuses on Jake Barnes, but on Jake in relation to Brett. The chapter begins with Jake's statement that he cannot remain outside the novel because he is too much involved in the people he will tell about . . . . "I made the unfortunate mistake, for a writer, of having first been Mr. Jake Barnes." He continues,

> The thing I would like to make whoever reads this believe, however incredible, is that such a passion and longing could exist in me for Brett Ashley that I would sometimes feel that it would tear me to pieces . . . . whenever I had just left Brett . . . I felt all of my world taken away, that it was all gone, even the shapes of things were changed, the trees and the houses and the fountains . . . . Brett Ashley could do that to me.

And the reason for Brett's power over Jake is also described: "she never lost her form. She was always clean bred, generous and her lines were always as sharp."

Brett as Hemingway hero is not implausible, particularly given the frustration of Jake Barnes' wound and the impossibility of what they both come to see as a lasting relationship. If their love resembles that between Nick and his sister Littless in "The Last Good Country," that too may be intentional. For Hemingway, the prototype of marriage was that tragic relationship between his parents. Their marriage appeared early in his fiction with "The Doctor and the Doctor's Wife" (a story virtually untouched from manuscript to publication), "Indian Camp," and in the magnificent house-cleaning scene of "Fathers and Sons." As he wrote in the manuscript version of that story,

. . . father was very nervous. He was married to a woman with whom he had
no more in common than a coyote has with a white French poodle . . . .[17]

And in an even earlier version, "a man suffers in his own home. There is
only one thing to do if a man is married to a woman with whom he has
nothing in common . . . and that is to get rid of her . . . Whoever, in a marriage of that sort, wins the first encounter is in command."

Marriage for Hemingway—at least fictionally—was never an ideal state.
Rather, his ideal seemed to be caught most effectively in the companionship
of man/woman, boy/girl, brother/sister—a relationship bound by caring
and sacrifice but not by obligation and power. Brett and Jake are, finally,
only companions—exiled as effectively from the people who accompany
them to Spain as if they were geographically alone. The geographical isolation Hemingway leaves for Littless and her brother, as he hides from the
game wardens for fishing out of season. A story of peril and macho brava-
do, "The Last Good Country" conveys the tender rapport between brother
and hero-worshipping little sister. It is also a story of Nick as initiator rather
than initiated. "We're partners," Littless says, as she accepts her brother as
guide and protector. Yet when Nick longs to kill the boy who turned him in,
he realizes that Littless's greater moral consciousness will protect him, will
keep him from harming anyone:

she can feel it because she is you sister and you love each other . . . .[18]

"The Last Good Country," though unfinished and hence never published until the Nick Adams stories were collected, also moves through
images, and one passage in particular gives the sense of Nick's love for Littless, his affinity with nature, and his admiration for personal qualities like
pride and grace:

They went along down the creek. Nick was studying the banks. He had seen
a mink's track and shown it to his sister and they had seen tiny ruby-crowned
kinglets that were hunting insects and let the boy and girl come close as they
moved sharply and delicately in the cedars. They had seen cedar waxwings so
calm and gentle and distinguished moving in their lovely elegance with the
magic wax touches on their wing coverts and their tails, and Littless had said,
"They're the most beautiful, Nickie. There couldn't be more simply beautiful
birds."
"They're built like your face," he said.
"No, Nickie, Don't make fun. Cedar waxwings make me so proud and
happy that I cry."
"When they wheel and light and then move so proud and friendly and gen-
tly . . ."[19]

It also works to create that image of Utopia that Hemingway will repeat
throughout his work—the undiscovered, untouched country (or sea); the
place free from corruption, malaise, personal dishonesty; the place clean
and well lighted; the place—whether geographical or anatomical—found

through initiative (travel, exploration, sexual discovery); the country that gives answers instead of only dilemmas.

The pervasive imagery begins here, in one of the few pieces of Hemingway's fiction which include a gentle and loving male and female relationship. But that there are few Hemingway stories in which male-female love is idyllic, that his second story collection was titled *Men Without Women*, lies less in his attitudes toward his women characters (at least in his early fiction) than in his characterization of male characters as adolescent, selfish, misdirected. There is evidence of much sympathy on Hemingway's part of the women he portrays in this early fiction, and his focus is not to narrow—to concentrate almost obsessively on the reflexive self—until after *A Farewell to Arms*. It is as if the young Hemingway believed in the romantic, mystic ideal of a genuine love, of a man's finding ultimate completion with a woman, until the catastrophe of his father's death. He saw that at least in part as a result of his mother's rigid incompatibility, her continuing lack of love. As he wrote in an unpublished essay,

> We are the generation whose fathers shot themselves. It is a very American thing to do and it is done, usually, when they lost their money although their wives are almost invariably a contributing cause. [20]

Hemingway's manuscripts show how constant was his concern for his father's suicide, as well as for his evident unhappiness before it. The draft of "Cross-Country Snow," for example, continues past the ending scene in the published story, with Mike asking, "What's the matter George?"

> "Oh the family," George said. "You know . . . Oh, I wish my father wasn't such a damn fool." [21]

Another unfinished story had as protagonist a boy named Edward Thompson who hates his mother and fights with kids who say that his father killed himself ("Suicide is a lonely way to die but it is least annoying to the family if there is some semblance of accident"). [22] "There are too many people alive for me to write about my father yet," he notes in the manuscript of "Fathers and Sons," and then continues:

> I loved him very much and I was fourteen before I knew that however he had made his life, I must make mine differently if I was to come through since his own life by then was ruined . . . . You could believe nothing your parents told you after a certain age because you had the example of their lives before you and you knew that whatever happened to your own life it should not be like that.

Marred, saddened, mistrustful of marriage because of his childhood experiences, Hemingway gave up most attempts to draw sympathetic women characters after he wrote the vehicle for expressing his own deep bereavement. *A Farewell to Arms* is not a romantic novel; it is instead a novel about loss. And the loss is that of his father, not of Catherine or a child. His notes on the manuscript of the novel express this transfer of emotion:

I loved my father. Very much . . . The novel was begun the winter of 1928 in Paris . . . that fall went to Chicago—saw my father—Drove to Key West with Sunny—she told me about my father—went to N.Y. to get Bumby—wrote father on train—informed of death in station—went to Chicago then to Kansas City to rewrite.[23]

Unable to trust that better experiences would be his, Hemingway transferred that emotion into some of the most powerful of his fiction—the loss of Santiago, of Robert Jordan, and particularly of Thomas Hudson in *Islands in the Stream*. It is Hudson who relinquishes all relationship with women, reaching humanity through his love for his sons—the male tie again reinforced. As Hudson thinks of his boys,

He had replaced everything except them with work and the steady hardworking life he had built on the island. That is, he thought he had. I would rather love a good house and the sea and my work than a woman, he thought. He knew it could never be true. But he could almost make it . . . .[24]

Truer than he may have known, Fitzgerald's words of analysis, that Hemingway had stopped listening to his women characters. In his early fiction, Hemingway's attention was on women as themselves. In the later novels and stories, because his attention had been usurped by the deaths of his father and other men, women characters exist primarily to give the Hemingway character another dimension. The angle of vision is skewed, oblique; it still reflects, but less accurately. And Robert Lowell's theory—that any good poet creates for us *his* world—is once again borne out: the last Hemingway world was utopian, full of seas and energy and words, but strangely devoid of women.

NOTES

1 F. Scott Fitzgerald, letter to Hemingway, Hemingway Collection, John F. Kennedy Library; used by permission of Collection.

2 Ernest Hemingway, *The Sun Also Rises* (New York: Charles Scribner's Sons, 1926), 60. Hereafter cited in text.

3 Ernest Hemingway, *In Our Time* (New York: Charles Scribner's Sons, 1925), 34, 35.

4 Manuscript version of "The End of Something," Hemingway Collection, Kennedy Library.

5 Ernest Hemingway, *Men Without Women* (New York: Charles Scribner's Sons, 1927), 39.

6 Manuscript version of "Hills Like White Elephants," Hemingway Collection, John F. Kennedy Library.

7 Early version begins: "The train moved through the hot valley. Fields of ripe grain started at the rails to stretch across the valley. Far off beyond the brown fields a line of trees grew along the course of the Ebro and beyond the river rose abruptly the mysterious white mountains.

"We had called them that as soon as we saw them. To be disgustingly accurate I had said, '*Look* at those god damn white mountains.'

"Hadley said, 'They are the most mysterious things I have ever seen.'

"They were white mountains, not white with snow or any artificial aid but white themselves furrowed and wrinkled by the rains like all good mountains and they were very wonderful strange shapes and there were two ranges of them, one on each side of the broad brown and green valley of the Ebro. On a cloudy dark day they might have been gray as a white elephant is gray in a circus tent, but in the July heat they shown white as white elephants in the sun . . . ."

8 On finished manuscript as if epigraph, Hemingway Collection, Kennedy Library.

9 Manuscript version of "Cat in the Rain," Hemingway Collection, Kennedy Library, pp. 8-9.

10 Epigraph to original *in our time* (Paris: Three Mountains Press, 1924), printed under title on title page.

11 Ernest Hemingway, *By-Line: Ernest Hemingway*, ed. William White (New York: Scribner's, 1967), 461.

12 Ernest Hemingway, "The Art of the Short Story," unpublished essay, Hemingway Collection, J. F. Kennedy Library, p. 4

13 Alan Holder, "The Other Hemingway," *Twentieth Century Literature* (1963), 153-57.

14 For example, see *Chicago Daily Tribune* (Nov. 27, 1926), p. 13; Herbert J. Muller, *Modern Fiction: A Study of Values* (New York: Funk & Wagnalls, 1937, pp. ·383-403); Henry Seidel Canby, *American Memoir* (Boston: Houghton Mifflin, 1947, pp. 339-44); R. W. Stallman, *The Houses That James Built and Other Literary Studies* (East Lansing, Mich.: Michigan State University Press 1961), 173-193; Sidney P. Moss, "Character, Vision, and Theme in *The Sun Also Rises*," *Iowa English Yearbook*, No. 9 (Fall, 1964), 64-67; and others.

15 Letter from F. Scott Fitzgerald, reprinted in "Fitzgerald's *Sun Also Rises*: Notes and Comments," *Fitzgerald/Hemingway Annual*, 1971, pp. 1-9.

16 *The Sun Also Rises* manuscript, Hemingway Collection, J. F. Kennedy Library.

17 Manuscript version, "Fathers and Sons," Hemingway Collection, Kennedy Library.

18 Ernest Hemingway, "The Last Good Country" in *The Nick Adams Stories*, ed. Philip Young (New York: Charles Scribner's Sons, 1972), 113.

19 *Ibid.*, 107-8.

20 From Hemingway's anti-Humanist essay, Item 811, Hemingway Collection, Kennedy Library.

21 Manuscript version of "Cross-Country Snow," Hemingway Collection, Kennedy Library.

22 Manuscript version of unpublished story about Edward Thomas, Hemingway Collection, Kennedy Library.

23 Manuscript of *A Farewell to Arms*, Hemingway's notes; Hemingway Collection, Kennedy Library.

24 Ernest Hemingway, *Islands in the Stream*, discarded manuscript, p. 16; Hemingway Collection, Kennedy Library.

HEMINGWAY'S POETRY:
ANGRY NOTES OF AN AMBIVALENT OVERMAN

Nicholas Gerogiannis

When I seek another word for music, I always find only the word Venice
. . . .

. . . .
My soul, a stringed instrument
sang to itself, invisibly touched,
a secret gondola song,
quivering with iridescent happiness.
—Did anyone listen to it?

Friedrich Nietzsche, Ecce Homo[1]

There is anger in Hemingway's poetry, but it is not the anger of an individual voice; this is the voice of an author unleashing the anger that is inherently part of his literary heritage. The messages in the poems are concentrated notes, which are merely a part of the more persistent anger that characterizes the fiction.[2] At times, Hemingway's anger is turned upon himself, and the poems reflect the depression caused by the author's ambivalence. At other times, his anger is directed at the world in which he lives. The assumptions which motivate him are those of an egoist; the judgments are those of a Nietzschean overman.

James Joyce identified egoist writing by making an important distinction. In his biography of Joyce, Richard Ellmann recounts an exchange that took place in 1908 between the author and his brother Stanislaus. Joyce's outburst is aimed at the psychological mode of writing:

"Psychologist! What can a man know but what passes inside his own head?" Stanislaus replied, "Then the psychological novel is an absurdity, you think? and the only novel is the egomaniac's? D'Annunzio's?" Joyce replied, "I said as much in my pamphlet."[3]

Joyce is referring to his 1901 essay "The Day of the Rabblement," which is a broadside against Irish parochialism. In this essay he lectures that until the artist "has freed himself from the mean influences about him," he is not an artist at all.[4] The examples that Joyce cites of the new literature are Flaubert's *Madame Bovary* and Gabriele D'Annunzio's *Il Fuoco* (*The Flame*, 1900).

A writer of egoist fiction employs many of the literary devices that the psychological novelist uses. However, there are distinguishing qualities. First, egoist writing is close in time and subject to the surface of life; this gives it a deceptive autobiographical quality. But to the egoist author experience is a fusion of the events of his own life with those things he has heard about, and those he has read. Thus his imagination places him within the living fictions created around his inspirations. Finally, following the precepts of Nietzsche, the literary goal of the egoist writer is not altruistic; although the egoist does seek to teach the community of sympathetic souls, his goal is to influence future generations. The egoist is an artist in the process of becoming, and he is usually a personality who impresses his legend upon his age. It is within this tradition that Hemingway belongs, along with Dante, Bryon, Stendhal, Flaubert, Turgeniev, Nietzsche, D'Annunzio, Joyce, and Pound.

Hemingway's path to Nietzsche is direct. Noel Fitch has documented the fact that on 4 May 1926 Hemingway left Shakespeare & Co. with James Gibbons Huneker's *Egoists: A Book of Supermen.* The central figures in Huneker's study are Stendhal and Nietzsche; Hemingway admired Stendhal, but on this occasion we must assume that he was interested in Nietzsche because, on 5 May, he returned to 12 rue de L'Odeon and checked out *Thus Spake Zarathustra.* [5]

Nietzsche scholar and translator Walter Kaufmann explains the idea of Nietzsche's hero: "The Overman is the man who has overcome himself; the passionate man who is the master of his passions; the creator who excels in both passion and reason and is able to employ his powers creatively." [6]

From this we see that there are many points where Nietzsche and Hemingway meet. Nietzsche built a powerful philosophy around the anger of his overman creator; Hemingway's work is an echo of that anger and that philosophy. Nietzsche and Hemingway would hardly have disagreed, for instance, on their feelings toward scholars. Hemingway probably approved of the martial quality with which Nietzsche imbued Zarathustra's aesthetics. Without question, Nietzsche's insistence on the idea of eternal recurrence was shared by Hemingway. He adopted Nietzsche's idea that a man and a woman could become one in a relationship—a sort of "overcouple." Most important, in his fiction and poetry, Hemingway dramatized and defended Zarathustra's insistence on the overman's right to "free death." [7]

All of this contains possibilities, but I would not presume to apply Nietzsche's philosophy to Hemingway's poetry, much less to his fiction and his life, if it were not for the discoveries which led me to consider Nietzsche in the first place.

By the time Hemingway encountered Zarathustra he had already been deeply influenced by a Nietzsche disciple, the Mediterranean overman—Gabriele D'Annunzio. Hemingway's poem "D'Annunzio" (p. 28) is a three-line verse that is meaningless when considered by itself; however, as I searched through Hemingway's writings, I was surprised to find that there are a number of overt and covert references to this Italian writer.

D'Annunzio was born in 1863, in Pescara, Italy. He established his reputation as a premier literary figure with a series of novels which particularly celebrated his relationships with aristocratic women. He was idolized. He became a figure very much like Lord Byron. In the mid 1890s he was deeply influenced by Richard Wagner and Nietzsche. He introduced the theme of the overman into Italy by adopting the principles of Nietzsche's creation to the Mediterranean man. In 1895, in Venice, he began his most celebrated love afair, with Eleonora Duse, the actress who was Sarah Bernhardt's only rival. D'Annunzio fused Nietzsche's philosophy, Wagner's influence, and the events of his relationship with Duse into his most famous novel, *The Flame*. Probably in 1918, but no later than 1920, Hemingway read *The Flame*.[8]

During the Great War D'Annunzio was the most famous man in Italy. In his critical biography *The Poet as Superman*, Anthony Rhodes summarizes D'Annunzio's military experience:

> His superiors soon lost trace of him and his exploits . . . . D'Annunzio delighted in a kind of individual enterprise in which, together with some chosen Ulyssean companions in a motor-boat, he would glide into an Austrian harbour by night, and fire off torpedoes, at shipping or at the shore . . . . Officially a commissioned officer in the army, he adopted on this own authority a naval title *Comandante* . . . . He fought in the air, on the sea, on the land . . . . His theory was that fear is natural to the body, and that courage to control it belongs to the mind.[9]

Obviously, there was much in D'Annunzio's style as a warrior for Hemingway to have admired, but there was also much about D'Annunzio that he rejected. In the four pages in *Across the River and Into the Trees* that are devoted to D'Annunzio,[10] we find passages that lead to extraordinary relationships between the writings and lives of these two men. In Hemingway's Venetian novel, Colonel Cantwell acknowledges that with D'Annunzio "it was always the same appearances."[11] And the Colonel offers a qualified homage: ". . . Lieutenant Colonel D'Annunzio, writer and national hero, certified and true if you must have heroes, and the Colonel did not believe in heroes . . ."[12]

As Hemingway moves Cantwell through Venice toward his rendezvous with Renata, he sends the reader an important message through his Colonel's thoughts and words. Cantwell is riding in a gondola past the house where D'Annunzio and Duse had lived. His remarks to his driver, Jackson, hold no qualifications for D'Annunzio as a writer:

> "Jackson," he said, "that small villa on the left belonged to Gabriele D'Annunzio, who was a great writer."
>
> "Yes, sir," said Jackson, "I'm glad to know about him. I never heard of him."
>
> "I'll check you out on what he wrote if you ever want to read him," the Colonel said. "There are some fair English translations."

"Thank you, sir," said Jackson. "I'd like to read him anytime I have time. He has a nice practical looking place. What did you say the name was?"

"D'Annunzio," the Colonel said. "Writer."

He added to himself, not wishing to confuse Jackson, nor to be difficult, as he had been with the man, several times that day, writer, poet, national hero, phraser of the dialectic of Fascism, macabre egotist, aviator, commander, or rider, in the first of the fast torpedo attack boats, Lieutenant Colonel of Infantry without knowing how to command a company, nor a platoon properly, the great, lovely writer of *Notturno* whom we respect, and jerk.[13]

The key phrase is "the great, lovely writer of *Notturno* whom we respect."

D'Annunzio wrote *Notturno*[14] in 1916 at his home in Venice while he was recuperating from a serious eye injury received in an airplane crash. In this lyrical memoir the author recalls his relationship with Duse; he exhibits a rare sense of remorse over having lost this greatest of all his lovers. He sentimentally recounts his military exploits with his comrades, and he recalls the death during battle of his closest wartime friends. He reflects on his life.

Notturno is written by a man in his fifties, a writer-turned-warrior, in pain and preparing himself to die while remembering his past. In spirit alone, D'Annunzio's memoir is close enough to *Across the River and Into the Trees* to be accepted as the prototype for Hemingway's novel. But there is more.

The central female figure in *Notturno* is D'Annunzio's daughter—Renata. She grew up adoring D'Annunzio, and prepared herself to serve him just as the heroines serve the heroes in his novels. Renata's sacrificing spirit pervades *Notturno* and constantly brings the author hope.

But Hemingway's Renata is not merely a fictional projection designed by the author to link himself to an old hero, and *Across the River and Into the Trees* is not merely Hemingway's *Notturno*. Hemingway's heroine, like her namesake, nurses her wounded hero and guides him through his ordeal. But Hemingway created his Renata by fusing D'Annunzio's daughter to D'Annunzio's fictional representation of his most celebrated mistress; Hemingway's Renata possesses the wisdom, sacrificing spirit, and erotic personality of the heroine of *The Flame*, La Foscarina, who is a thinly-disguised persona for Eleonora Duse. Thus Hemingway achieved the satisfaction of entering a lyrical and erotic myth. Cantwell's thoughts reflect this romantic projection:

> But now he was passing the house where the poor beat-up old boy had lived with his great, sad, and never properly loved actress, and he thought of her wonderful hands, and her so transformable face, that was not beautiful, but that gave you all love, glory, and delight and sadness; and of the way the curve of her fore-arm could break your heart, and he thought, Christ they are dead and I do not know where either one is buried even. But I certainly hope they had fun in that house.[15]

Most of Cantwell's thoughts are of the woman, and his memory of Eleonora Duse is remarkable for its sympathetic insight.

The structure of *Across the River and Into the Trees* parallels in many respects the structure of *The Flame*. It is important to note that the heroes of both novels define themselves through references to historical figures. (D'Annunzio's hero, Stelio Effrena, is imbued with the author's sense of himself as the heir to Dante; naturally, Dante is prominent in Hemingway's novel.) Both strong men, D'Annunzio's Stelio and Hemingway's Richard, are baptised in the font of experience and art—that font is Venice. In *The Flame*, Stelio pays homage to his spiritual master, Wagner, by stopping his gondola and placing flowers before the dying man's door; in *Across the River and Into the Trees*, Cantwell rides in his gondola past D'Annunzio's door, remembers, and offers his best wishes across time.

There is an important turnabout between the characters of the two novels. D'Annunzio's novel is about a love affair between an older woman and a younger man; Hemingway's novel is about an older man and a younger woman. D'Annunzio's hero and Hemingway's heroine play similar roles in their respective novels; both are young people who learn from their older lovers, and they envy them their experience. Also, the roles of the two older characters, D'Annunzio's Foscarina and Hemingway's Cantwell, are similar. Cantwell shares with Foscarina (Duse) a deep symbolic association with Venice, a history of pain and pleasure, and a majestic sadness.

Duse, or at least Foscarina of *The Flame*, must have left a deep impression on Hemingway's youthful imagination in 1918. Duse was six years older than D'Annunzio; the author of *The Flame* continuously reminds the reader of the age difference between Stelio and Foscarina in order to dramatize his hero's power over this erotic and experienced woman. Hemingway could not have missed applying this to his "affair" with Agnes von Kurowsky. His romantic remembrances of his time in Italy may have been influenced by *The Flame*.[16] Agnes was seven years older than Hemingway. Katy Smith, with whom he had an ambiguous relationship in Chicago, was also seven years older than he was. Hadley Richardson was eight years older. We must wonder whether the conquest of an older woman had not become a romantic ideal for him, a D'Annunzian ideal.

Foscarina (Duse) has qualities which remind us of Catherine Barkley and *A Farewell to Arms*. In 1929, F. Scott Fitzgerald suggested this same point in a letter to Hemingway:

> You are seeing him Frederic in a sophisticated way as now you see yourself then but you're still seeing her as you did in 1917 through a 19-year-old's eyes—in consequence unless you make her a bit fatuous occasionally the contrast jars—either the writer is a simple fellow or she is Elenora [sic] Duse disguised as a Red Cross nurse.[17]

Fitzgerald had read the typescript of *A Farewell to Arms*, and he sent Hemingway a not entirely welcome set of criticisms and suggestions. In this case, Fitzgerald made a rather fine critical leap with his insignt about Catherine Barkley and Duse (one that possibly could have been made only by another novelist).

Foscarina (Duse) feels "a great solitude," a separateness from others. During moments when her terror of loneliness and death overwhelm her, she is driven further within herself and she struggles against her lover. Wherever the lovers go, Foscarina is associated with statues, which are "witnesses to her own decay."[18] Eventually, she attempts to lose herself in a sense of oneness with the hero.

Foscarina's past loves and mystery appeal to the hero of The Flame, who dreams of "extraordinary promiscuities."[19] Their affair begins quickly. But Foscarina draws Stelio close to her because she discovers "his secret need of believing and confiding."[20] The heroine's previous affairs and experiences have been annulled (although they occasionally seem to bother the hero). Through her love for Stelio, Foscarina recovers her "carnal power." She offers her lover her "girlhood's dream intact, the dream of Juliet."[21] Like Eleonora Duse, Foscarina had played the part of Juliet when she was fourteen, and from that mystical evening in her past her "destiny seemed to be getting mixed up with the destiny of the Veronese maiden."[22] To consummate her love for Stelio she asks only one thing: "A child by you."[23]

D'Annunzio defines the overman's woman as "a good and faithful instrument at the service of genius, a strong, willing companion."[24] This portrait of the overman's lover describes many of Hemingway's heroines; this idealized image—a sacrificing spirit linked to an erotic sensibility—caused him trouble. But I believe that Eleonora Duse's myth, through D'Annunzio's fictional heroine, was the inspiration for Hemingway's ideal woman. His romantic heroines—Catherine, Maria, Renata—are women with experience, and they are good sexual mates for his heroes, who have "a secret need for believing and confiding."

The poems which deal with Hemingway's relationships with women reveal a man who compromises his ideal of independence in order to satisfy his complex vulnerability and his needs for domesticity; repeatedly this leads him to personal failure and remorse. At first, a woman's sense of freedom appealed to Hemingway as it did to D'Annunzio. The Dionysian "Lines to a Young Lady on Her Having Very Nearly Won a Vögel" contains the D'Annunzian image of the "two sleepy birds" as background to the woman dancing with "pagan grace" (p. 33). But following the preliminary enticement, things become complex. The woman in "Bird of Night" (p. 36) is a predator/lover, much like Foscarina who is described as a "bird of prey." In this poem, the sense of erotic sanctuary is achieved through a D'Annunzian mixture of strong nature and sexual images. The man escapes from solitude beneath the "pinions" of his "bird of night" much like Frederick Henry seeks his sanctuary beneath the tent of Catherine's hair. There is pain in this kind of love. Colonel Cantwell feels "how close life comes to death when there is ecstasy."[25]

Hemingway dramatizes this intimately in "Killed Piave — July 8 — 1918," which links the date of his wounding to the image of a nocturnal lover who is described as "A dull, cold, rigid bayonet/On my hot-swollen, throbbing soul" (p. 35). However, in other poems written in Chicago during 1920-1921, the city inhibits sensuality. Hemingway's Dionysian dreams were complicated by his domestic impulses. In "Night comes with soft and drowsy plumes . . . " (p.31) and "At night I lay with you . . . " (p. 32) we sense a prelude to domesticity. In "On Weddynge Gyftes" (p. 38), an exaggerated and ironic statement on antiquated wedding rituals, he feels conformity and domesticity closing in on him. The voice in the facetious "I'm off'n wild wimmen . . . " (p. 57) is howling toward domesticity.

In a sharp brief scene early in *The Flame* D'Annunzio characterizes domestic bliss as an anesthetic condition for those who are unconscious and dumb.[26] His hero prefers the drama of his affair with his "carnal mistress." As D'Annunzio seems to interpret Nietzsche, after lovers achieve their sense of oneness, the man is free, carnally, to move on. This is what happens in *The Flame*, and this is what D'Annunzio did countless times throughout his life. Hemingway used death as a device to end the oneness achieved by his lovers in *A Farewell to Arms* and *For Whom the Bell Tolls*. At other times in his fiction, as in his life, matters were not so conveniently arranged. In the poem "Sequel," written about the time Ernest left Hadley, indecision has turned into self-pity: "So if she dies/And if you write about it/Being a writer and a shit/Dulling it so you sleep again at night" (p. 91). "We leave them all quite easily/When dislike overcomes our love" (p. 121), Hemingway writes in "Black-Ass Poem After Talking to Pamela Churchill." "Travel Poem" (p. 124) also reflects the dark side of a relationship when domesticity is felt to be an irritant. D'Annunzio consciously and successfully acted out his Dionysian roles; he left them all quite easily. Hemingway's rather fantastic bragging about his sexual exploits suggests that at times he may have envied D'Annunzio's erotic life.

Cantwell reflects on D'Annunzio as a warrior and a lover. D'Annunzio "had moved through the different arms of the service as he had moved in and out of the arms of different women. All the arms were pleasant that D'Annunzio served with and the mission was fast and easily over, except the infantry"[27] The repetition and double usage of the world "arms" should attract our attention, because by this point in *Across the River and Into the Trees* Hemingway has made other plays on worlds. After all, Cantwell, through his memorial service at the spot where he was wounded in World War I, has been linked to Hemingway and to the hero of *A Farewell to*

Arms. The Colonel's thoughts, through a reference to D'Annunzio, form another link between Hemingway's Italian novels:

> And the Colonel remembered one time when he had stood, commanding a platoon of assault troops, while it was raining in one of the interminable winters, when the rain fell always; or at least, always when there were parades or speeches to the troops, and d'Annunzio . . . looking thirty hours dead, was shouting, "Morire non è basta," and the Colonel, then a lieutenant, had thought, "What the muck more do they want of us?"[28]

This sounds like a scene which Frederic Henry describes in *A Farewell to Arms*:

> I was alwasy embarrassed by the words sacred, glorious, and sacrifice and the expression in vain. We had heard them, sometimes standing in the rain almost out of earshot, so that only the shouted words came through, and had read them, on proclamations . . .[29]

The patriotic oration delivered during an "interminable winter" sounds like the occasion in November 1917 when D'Annunzio addressed the army at Piave.[30] It was a memorable scene which Hemingway could have heard about when he arrived in the region seven months later. On that occasion D'Annunzio stirred the simple hearts of his audience by applying religious symbolism and images to the task that the soldiers faced. In June 1918 an American public information officer asked D'Annunzio to write a poem in salute to the Fourth of July.[31] To commemorate Americans' involvement in the war D'Annunzio wrote a sixty-stanza ode "All' America in Armi" ("To America in Arms"); the poem was translated into English by B. Harvey Carroll, American Consul at Venice, and it was published in Milan's *Corriere della Sera* on 4 July 1918, four days before Hemingway was wounded. This may be one of the "proclamations" that Frederic Henry had read. "To America in Arms" is filled with words that he finds "obscene." When Frederic says his farewell to arms, he is declaring his freedom from the sentiments contained in D'Annunzio's poem.

Hemingway's poem "To Good Guys Dead" also bitterly denounces the patriotic sentiments and heroic words that only resulted in dead soldiers: "Patriotism,/Democracy,/Honor—/Words and phrases,/They either bitched or killed us" (p. 47). "Champs d'Honneur" depicts a view of the Great War that is far different from D'Annunzio's heroic style: "Soldiers smother in a ditch;/Choking through the whole attack" (p. 27). "Shock Troops" (p. 43) defines the difference between jovial fresh recruits and veterans. "Riparto d'Assalto" (p. 46) presents a contrast between the sexual fantasies of a non-combatant lieutenant and an ambulance full of mortally wounded Arditi. "Arsiero, Asiago . . . " (p. 49) is about "all the places where men died that nobody ever heard about."[32] "All armies are the same . . . " (p. 42) describes the men who are entrapped by the war; there is little sense of D'Annunzian adventure in it for them.

Although Hemingway reacted against D'Annunzio's easy language of war, he evidently embraced D'Annunzio's legend and the forms he used to achieve it. Gabriele D'Annunzio was fifty-two years old when Italy entered the war. He was a free lance, a legendary figure who believed in himself. An impressionable eighteen when he arrived in Italy, Hemingway's youthful personality was influenced by D'Annunzio's style of martial romanticism. Much of D'Annunzio's poetry, like his "To a Torpedo-boat in the Adriatic,"[33] was written in honor of his military exploits and for the men who served with him in his often unauthorized adventures. But that was World War I, and D'Annunzio was in the Italian army. In World War II, the American army in Europe had little patience with a middle-aged writer's extracurricular activities in the business of war. Hemingway was out of his time. His attempt at a D'Annunzian adventure in the Caribbean aboard the *Pilar* ended with a whimper. Before he dramatized the experience in *Islands in the Stream*, he lamented his fate in "First Poem to Mary in London": "His boat is in the faraway sea. His people are dispersed and his armaments surrendered to the proper authorities. Duly receipted and accounted for" (p. 103). Although Hemingway's heroes reject D'Annunzio's language, Hemingway embraces and defends the concepts of honor and courage in his World War II poems.

Long before Hemingway found himself out of time in his last war, he reacted to threats from other enemies—critics and scholars. He reacted sharply, in a typically Nietzschean fashion. In his story-essay "A Natural History of the Dead" Hemingway imagines "indecorous" deaths for Humanist critics, these "children of decorous cohabitation."[34] He had considered the same group in "Poem, 1928":

> They say it's over
> The need, now, is for order
> Not for substance
> For piety
> We must be full of grace, or on the way there,
> Our works must lead to something,
> Morally instructive, dull, but stemming from
> the classics
> Which mostly dealt, if I remember,
> With incest, rapes, and wars
> And dirty stories
> My Ovid, James, where is it got to— (p. 95)

Hemingway was reacting to what he sensed to be an academic attempt to reduce the experiences of his generation to an abstraction. Zarathustra's words on his enemies, the scholars, must have given Hemingway joy: "I have freedom and the air over the fresh earth; rather would I sleep on ox-hides than on their decorums and respectabilities."[35] Hemingway concludes "Poem, 1928" with a Nietzschean denunciation:

> We have something that cannot be taken from us by an
>   article
> Nor abolished by a critical agreement of Professors
> The searchers for order will find that there is a certain
>   discipline in the acceptance of experience.
> They may, that is;
> They rarely find out anything they cannot read in
>   books or articles
> But if we last and are not destroyed
> And we are durable because we have lasted. We do
>   not destroy easily.
> We'll write the books.
> They will not read them
> But their children may
> If they have children. (p. 96)

Hemingway's argument is weak and abstract because of its bluntness. In order to understand this clash between two systems of value we need the egoist voice of Ezra Pound:

> Christ follows Dionysius,
> Phallic and ambrosial
> Made way for macerations;
> Caliban casts out Ariel.[36]

Dionysius represents the highest form of faith for the egoist/overman. Kaufmann explains that to Nietzsche, Dionysius "represents passion controlled and creatively employed as opposed to the negation of the passions, of the body and of the world."[37] But self-overcoming is a challenge, not a prediction; whoever chooses the way of the overman creator chooses a lonely path. In *The Birth of Tragedy* and *Beyond Good and Evil*, Nietzsche explains that ambiguity is part of the very nature of the Dionysian artist. In a letter to his sister, he alludes to his own life, saying the overman must "strike new paths, fighting the habitual, experiencing the insecurity of independence and the frequent wavering of one's feelings and even one's conscience . . . ."[39] Like the character in "Chapter VII" of *In Our Time,* the persona in Hemingway's poem "Chapter Heading" seems to believe in Nietzsche during the day and Christ during the night:

> For we have thought the longer thoughts
>   And gone the shorter way.
> And we have danced to devils' tunes,
>   Shivering home to pray;
> To serve one master in the night,
>   Another in the day. (p. 34)

D'Annunzio announced the principle of self-reliance for the overman creator in his poem *Maia*:

> You must know you are the lone one of your species,
> For in your march through life you are alone,
> Alone at the last supreme moment,
> Alone you are the strongest friend you have.[39]

Hemingway passes on this idea to Adriana Ivancich in "Lines to a Girl 5 Days After Her 21st Birthday." His echo of Kipling—"She travels the fastest/Who travels alone" (p. 125)—underscores his message to Adriana that the artist's life is perverted and weakened by relationships; there is decay in contacts. What is important is the creator's sense of himself, of his overcoming through hard work. Hemingway challenges the young artist to "Live alone and like it/Like it for a day" (p. 125). When she misunderstands his meaning, his clarification defines the personal relationships of every true overman artist: "But I will not *be* alone, angrily she said. / Only in your heart, he said. Only in your head" (pp. 125-126). He accepts her right to be superior, but he urges her to go beyond argument to action—to work and to struggle. But above all, he tells her, "Please *do* it your own way" [emphasis Hemingway's].

> Trade bed for a pencil
> Trade sorrow for a page
> No work it out your own way
> Have good luck at your age. (p. 126)

He could have added Zarathustra's words to the creator: "But the worst enemy you can encounter will alway be you, yourself; you lie in wait for yourself in caves and woods."[40]

Zarathustra counsels us to "Remain faithful to the earth, and do not believe those who speak to you of otherworldly hopes."[41] "Eternal recurrence," writes Kaufmann, " . . . is an antithesis to the Christian conception of time and history."[42] Nietzsche teaches us that for man to overcome his human self, to become overman, he must have the guidance of a model, an "educator." The passing on, from generation to generation, of the challenge to become overman is part of what Nietzsche calls "eternal recurrence." Nietzsche looked to Wagner; D'Annunzio looked to Wagner and Nietzsche; Joyce looked to Flaubert and D'Annunzio; Hemingway looked to D'Annunzio, Pound, and Joyce. D'Annunzio concludes *The Flame* with Wagner's death and a speech by his hero that sounds like a modern sequel to *Ecclesiastes*; immediately following, Stelio leaves to accompany the hero's casket back to Germany. Hemingway's faith in the earth is legend; however, it is still surprising to many people that he was an "educator." He was well aware of his role. No other writer of this century, except Pound perhaps, set out as consciously as Hemingway did to influence the sensibilities of the children in the coming generations. I know only that in May 1926

Hemingway walked out of Shakespeare and Company carrying *Thus Spake Zarathustra*, and that he kept the book until September; however, the more I learn about Nietzsche's book the more I am convinced that Hemingway's fictions are dramatizations of Zarathustra's teachings, and Hemingway's life was that of an ambivalent overman.

Now we must recall Zarathustra's final lesson to his children: get along without me.

After the flame has been passed, all that is left is the wish for "a worthy end."[43] "Many die too late, and a few die too early. The doctrine still sounds strange: 'Die at the right time!' "[44] Thus, Zarathustra counsels us on "free death." In *The Flame*, the dying of Wagner casts a spell over the entire story. D'Annunzio's hero is established as Wagner's spiritual disciple; after an encounter with the stricken hero, Stelio is inspired to an epiphany of his highest aesthetics and concludes with a consideration of Wagner: "He has conquered; he may die."[45] The words reflect the belief Hemingway expresses in his "Poem to Miss Mary": "IF your dues are paid/You carry, always, your own spade" (p. 119).

The notion of heroic suicide, or "free death," is central to some of Hemingway's more important poems, as it is to much of his prose. "Montparnasse" contrasts the lonely suicides of transients with the histrionics of "the people one knows" (p. 50) who spend their afternoons in Paris cafes. Dorothy Parker, who "always vomitted in time" (p. 87), is attacked in "To a Tragic Poetess" for her sham suicide attempts and for her using the occasions as material for her poems. Hemingway characterizes her as being devoid of sympathetic imagination:

> To sit one day in the Luticia
> and joke about a funeral passing in the rain
> It gave no pain
> because you did not know the people. (p. 87)

For real tragedy, Hemingway turns to the "suicides of sunny Spain" (p. 89). He recounts the delirious despair suffered by the bullfighters Litri (Manuel Baez) and Maera (Manuel Garcia) before they died. The poetic anecdote of the methodical suicide of an eighty-year-old man in Miguelete sounds like the truth that was left out of "A Clean, Well-Lighted Place":

> An old man named Valentin Magarza
> climbed in his eightieth year the tower of Miguelete
> and was, the Valencian paper said,
> destroyed completely on the pavement.
> His granddaughter had said he was a bother
> and he was getting old. (p. 88)

It took Nietzsche eleven years to die following the destruction of his mind. D'Annunzio tempted death repeatedly during the Great War; however, his fate was to sink into old age and silence behind dark veils of privacy at his villa which had belonged to Wagner's daughter. Hemingway's last true heroic gesture was the wartime adventure aboard the *Pilar*. Following that he joined the world war in Europe. In "First Poem to Mary in London" he writes: "No, it is not a good ending. Not the ending we had hoped for . . . . Not as we thought it should be each time we took her from harbour" (p. 104).

The lassitude remained when he began to write again. In the last 1940's, Hemingway returned in his imagination and in his fiction to the Italy of his youth. He revisited old places and old fictions. After the Great War, when it had seemed to him that D'Annunzio placed personal glory before the deaths of 500,000 Italian soldiers, he had called him a "son of a bitch" (p. 28). D'Annunzio got mixed up in politics (which is anathema to an overman creator), but Hemingway still believed in 1923 that the old hero would topple Mussolini. He prophesied in "Mussolini: Biggest Bluff in Europe": "A new opposition will rise, it is forming already, and it will be lead by that old, bald-headed, perhaps a little insane but thoroughly sincere, divinely brave swashbuckler, Gabriele D'Annunzio."[46] D'Annunzio disappointed him and Italy. Thus, Cantwell calls him a "jerk,"[47] which he later defines as "a man who has never worked at his trade (oficio) truly, and is presumptuous in some annoying way."[48] In 1950, to vent his frustration over the critical and public reception of *Across the River and Into the Trees*, Hemingway recorded "In Harry's Bar in Venice."[49] This tale of an eighteen-year-old colonel who is in love with an eighty-six-year-old Venetian countess, but who finally falls for a Venetian maiden, is for the most part a parody of *The Flame*, not of *Across the River and Into the Trees*. Just before recording this extemporaneous concoction, he told A. E. Hotchner: "The parody is the last refuge of the frustrated writer."[50] In this case I am not sure whether Hemingway was denying an old story he had loved, and thus denying the influence of its author, by mocking them, or whether he was using a crude form to send a message to anyone who was listening—the same message he had tried to send in his Venetian novel. Or, perhaps, supported by the wine, Hemingway was just weaving a nocturnal entertainment for himself.

But I am sure that for more than thirty years of Ernest Hemingway's life Eleonora Duse was his muse, and that at least for his Italian novels, his true Penelope was D'Annunzio.

NOTES

1 Friedrich Nietzsche, *Ecce Homo*, in *Basic Writings of Nietzsche*, tr. and ed. Walter Kaufmann (New York: Modern Library, 1968), p. 708.

2 Ernest Hemingway, *88 Poems*, ed. Nicholas Gerogiannis (New York: Harcourt Brace Jovanovich/Bruccoli Clark, 1979). All subsequent references to Hemingway's poems will be to this edition.

3 Richard Ellmann, *James Joyce* (New York: Oxford University Press, 1959), p. 275.

4 James Joyce, "The Day of the Rabblement," in *The Critical Writings of James Joyce*, ed. Ellsworth Mason and Richard Ellmann (New York: Viking, 1964), p. 71.

5 Noel Fitch, "C/O Shakespeare and Company," *Fitzgerald/Hemingway Annual 1977* (Detroit: Gale Research 1977), p. 176.

6 W[alter] K[aufman]n, "Friedrich Nietzsche," *Encyclopaedia Britannica*, 1966, Vol. 16, p. 496. For the sake of brevity and directness I have selected to cite Kaufmann's *Britannica* entry. His introductions and notes to *The Portable Nietzsche* (cited below) and to *Basic Writings of Nietzsche* (cited above), as well as his classic study *Nietzsche: Philosopher, Psychologist, Antichrist* (Princeton, N. J.: Princeton University Press, 1950), contain the same definitions in more detailed form.

7 Friedrich Nietzsche, *Thus Spoke Zarathustra*, in *The Portable Nietzsche*, ed. and tr. Walter Kaufmann (1954; rpt. New York: Penguin, 1978), pp. 183-186.

8 Carlos Baker, *Ernest Hemingway: A Life Story* (New York; Scribner's, 1969), p. 69. Baker writes that in March 1920, Hemingway gave an inscribed copy of *The Flame* to Dorothy Connable. More information on this and related readings of D'Annunzio's works is forthcoming in Michael Reynolds' *Hemingway's Reading, 1910-1940* (Princeton University Press).

9 Anthony Rhodes, *The Poet as Superman: A Life of Gabriele D'Annunzio* (London: Weidenfeld and Nicolson, 1959), p. 157. For my account of D'Annunzio's life I have relied on Rhodes and the following biographies:
Tom Antongini, *D'Annunzio* (London: Heinemann, 1938). Reynolds reports that in May 1938 Hemingway ordered this biography from Scribner's bookstore.
Phillipe Julian, *D'Annunzio*, tr. Stephen Hardman (New York: Viking, 1973).
Frances Winwar, *Wingless Victory: A Biography of Gabriele D'Annunzio and Eleonora Duse* New York: Harper and Brothers, 1956).

10 Ernest Hemingway, *Across the River and Into the Trees* (New York: Scribner's, 1950), pp. 49-52.

11 *Across the River and Into the Trees*, p. 50.

12 *Across the River and Into the Trees*, p. 50.

13 *Across the River and Into the Trees*, pp. 51-52.

14 Gabriele D'Annunzio, *Notturno* (Milano: Presso I. Fratelli Treves, 1922). Since Hemingway refers to the book by its Italian title, I assume that he read the above edition or a later reprint; however, he could have read the French translation: Gabriele D'Annunzio, *Nocturne* (Paris: Calmann-Levy, 1923).

15 *Across the River and Into the Trees*, p. 51.

16 Catherine Barkley's emotional and erotic personality cannot be explained away by comparing her to Agnes von Kurowsky. The Agnes that Michael Reynold reveals in *Hemingway's First War: The Making of "A Farewell to Arms"* (Princeton: Princeton University Press, 1976), and in "The Agnes Tapes: A Farewell to Catherine Barkley," *Fitzgerald/Hemingway Annual 1979* (Detroit: Gale/Bruccoli Clark, 1980), pp. 251-276, is not essentially the sexual Catherine of *A Farewell to Arms*. Hadley may be closer in that respect. Perhaps Foscarina (Duse) is closest of all.

17 *Hemingway's First War*, pp. 18-19.
18 Gabriele D'Annunzio, *The Flame of Life*, tr. Baron Gustavo Tosti (New York: Collier, n.d.), p. 267. I have found three English translations of *The Flame* (sometimes translated as *The Flame of Life*). All are quite similar. I have selected this edition for reference purposes because it may be the easiest to locate.
19 *The Flame of Life*, p. 107.
20 *The Flame of Life*, p. 176.
21 *The Flame of Life*, p. 328.
22 *The Flame of Life*, p. 320.
23 *The Flame of Life*, p. 326.
24 *The Flame of Life*, p. 396.
25 *Across the River and Into the Trees*, p. 219.
26 *The Flame of Life*, pp. 116-120.
27 *Across the River and Into the Trees*, p. 49.
28 *Across the River and Into the Trees*, p. 50.
29 Ernest Hemingway, *A Farewell to Arms* (New York: Scribner's, 1929), p. 196.
30 *Wingless Victory*, pp. 287-288.
31 *Wingless Victory*, p. 290. Also see Carl A. Swanson, "D'Annunzio's Ode 'All' America in Armi' (IV Luglio MCMXVIII)," *Italica* (Sept. 1953): 135-143.
32 Quoted from *Hemingway's First War*, p. 14.
33 George R. Kay, ed., *The Penguin Book of Italian Verse* (1958; rpt. Middlesex, England: Penguin, 1968), p. 338.
34 Ernest Hemingway, "A Natural History of the Dead," in *Death in the Afternoon* (1932; rpt. New York: Scribner's, 1972), p. 139. A reference to Humanists was cut in an early draft of "Poem, 1928"; see *88 Poems*, p. 94.
35 *Thus Spoke Zarathustra*, p. 237.
36 Hugh Selwyn Mauberley, *Personae: The Collected Shorter Poems of Ezra Pound* (New York: New Directions, 1926), p. 189.
37 Kaufmann, "Friedrich Nietzsche," p. 496.
38 *The Portable Nietzsche*, p. 29.
39 Quoted in *The Poet as Superman*, p. 52.
40 *Thus Spoke Zarathustra*, p. 176.
41 *Thus Spoke Zarathustra*, p. 125.
42 Kaufmann, "Friedrich Nietzsche," p. 496.
43 *The Flame of Life*, p. 195.
44 *Thus Spoke Zarathustra*, p. 183.
45 *The Flame of Life*, p. 222.
46 Ernest Hemingway, "Mussolini: Biggest Bluff in Europe," *The Toronto Daily Star* (January 27, 1923) reprinted in *By-Line: Ernest Hemingway*, ed. William White (New York: Scribner's, 1967), p. 65.
47 *Across the River and Into the Trees*, p. 52.
48 *Across the River and Into the Trees*, p. 97.
49 *Ernest Hemingway Reading*, Caedmon (TC 1185).
50 *Ernest Hemingway Reading*, quoted on back cover.

HEMINGWAY OF *THE STAR*

Scott Donaldson

If Hemingway had stuck to his trade as a reporter, Philip Young remarked in his foreword to *Byline: Ernest Hemingway,* he "would have ranked among the best there ever were."[1] The reviewers of *Byline* did not go that far, but they generally admired Hemingway's articles in the *Toronto Star* papers, the *Daily Star* and its feature-oriented Saturday supplement, the *Star Weekly*, for their freshness and wit and liveliness. These newspaper pieces, written from 1920 to 1923, were remarkably personal for a profession which lays claim to objectivity. In writing about what he saw and heard and learned on his pan-atlantic beat, Hemingway of *The Star* "put his personality, his tastes, even his prejudices into his articles."[2] That was fine with his employers. What *The Star* wanted from him was color, and it was color he supplied.[3]

When he first began contributing features to the *Toronto Star* in the winter of 1920, young Hemingway had already benefited from an apprenticeship on one of the great American newspapers, the *Kansas City Star*. During his seven months in Kansas City in 1917 and 1918, he absorbed the principles of the paper's style sheet, which advised reporters to write short sentences in vigorous English and to avoid extravagant adjectives. He also acquired in Lionel Moise a star newspaperman in the *Front Page* mold to emulate. Cub reporter Hemingway, only weeks out of Oak Park high school, took to following Moise around, and for once his admiration lasted. "Lionel Moise was a great re-write man," his reminiscence in the Kennedy Library begins.

> He could carry four stories in his head and go to the telephone and take a fifth and then write all five at full speed to catch an edition. There would be something alive about each one. He was always the highest paid man on every paper he worked on. If any other man was getting more money he quit or had his pay raised.
>
> He never spoke to the other reporters unless he had been drinking. He was tall and thin and had long arms and big hands. He was the fastest man on a typewriter I ever knew. He drove a motor car [this was 1917, remember] and it was understood that a woman had given it to him. One night she stabbed him in it out on the Lincoln highway halfway to Jefferson City. He took the knife away from her and threw it out of the car. Then he did something awful to her. She was lying in the back of the car when they found them. Moise drove the car all the way in to Kansas City with her fixed that way.[4]

Here Hemingway celebrates the old-style reporter not just for his eccentricity and toughness, but also for his skill. Moise was fast, he could carry five stories in his head and get them down on paper under pressure, and he could contribute something of his own to every story, something that made it come "alive." That was what Hemingway was after, too.

Early in 1920 Hemingway began haunting the *Toronto Star* news room so ubiquitously that J. Herbert Cranston, editor of the *Star Weekly*, finally put him on a space rate basis. That was a cheap arrangement for the paper, which only paid for what it wanted to print and not very much, either: half a cent to a penny a word for the features they ran beginning February 14, 1920. Within a month, however, Cranston raised Hemingway's psychic income by awarding him his first byline. The editor appreciated the young free-lancer's gift for humor, or really for satire broad enough to appeal to the paper's middle-class readers.[5] The *Star* ran fifteen pieces between February and May, when Hemingway went back to Chicago. Even at that distance, he continued to supply the *Star Weekly* with occasional features. Cranston liked his stuff, and so did John R. Bone, the *Star's* managing editor. In February 1921 he wrote Hemingway suggesting a regular job.

Before replying Hemingway consulted his friend Gregory Clark, the features editor of the paper, and got some bad advice. Clark told him to ask for $90 a week (which would have made him the highest paid reporter on the paper, including Clark) since the *Daily Star* wanted him "hard." "The chief wants men to jazz up the paper," Clark explained. "He hasn't any. He thinks of you." At the time Hemingway was earning $40 a week in Chicago as assistant editor of the *Cooperative Commonwealth*, a slick-paper monthly extolling the doubtful virtues of the Co-operative Society of America. In responding to Bone he inflated that salary somewhat. "At the present I am making $75.00 a week at agreeable, though rather dull work," he wrote the *Star's* managing editor in March. "I would be glad to come with you at $85.00 a week and could report April 1."[6]

That proposal elicited only silence, but Clark had another scheme in mind. The rumor was that Cranston would be hired away by the *Toronto Sunday World*. If Cranston left he'd take Clark with him and Hemingway would be getting an offer too. That shift did not materialize, however, and late in October, now a married man without any job at all (he'd quit the *Cooperative Commonwealth* when it became clear that the society it was supposed to promote, having fleeced its members, was going into bankruptcy), Hemingway began another letter to Bone. "You very kindly suggested . . . a position last February," he reminded him, "but at that time I was getting some valuable experience and a very satisfactory salary here . . . and in answering your letter named a salary figure which was more, I believe, than you wished to pay."[7] Either that note, or some other communication to Toronto, struck fire. By the Monday after Thanksgiving it was arranged that Hemingway should go to Paris as a roving correspondent for both *Star* papers, to be paid at regular space rates and expenses on most stories but at $75 a week and expenses when covering specific assignments.[8]

As Charles Fenton pointed out in his valuable book on *The Apprenticeship of Ernest Hemingway*, the young writer was lucky to go overseas under the sponsorship of the *Toronto Star*, which gave him virtually unlimited freedom in choosing material and expected in return "lively, entertaining dispatches, intimate and subjective." By contrast, the European bureau of one of the major American papers would have required much more routine factual reporting and permitted much less personal latitude.[9] Given his head, Hemingway cultivated his satirical bent, writing pieces at the expense of phony would-be artists, thrill-seeking tourists, venal Frenchmen, and rude Germans.

He met the other foreign correspondents in Paris, made friends with a couple of them, notably Guy Hickok, but he clearly saw himself as different. One distinction was that he was also getting acquainted with the literary community in Paris, including Gertrude Stein and Ezra Pound. He regarded serious writing, not journalism, as his real profession. In an unpublished sketch which may have been originally intended for *A Moveable Feast*, Hemingway used the length of his unbarbered hair as a symbol of the difference.

> As long as I did newspaper work and had to go to different parts of Europe on assignments it was necessary to have one presentable suit, go to the barbers, and have one pair of respectable shoes. These were a liability when I was trying to write because they made it possible to leave your own side of the river and go over to the right bank to see your friends there, go to the races and do all the things that were fun that you could not afford or that got you into trouble. I found out very quickly that the best way to avoid going over to the right bank and get involved in all the pleasant things that I could not afford and that left me with, at the least, gastric remorse was not to get a haircut. You could not go over to the right bank with your hair cut like one of those wonderful Japanese noblemen painters who were friends of Ezra's . . .

> Sometimes I would run into foreign correspondents I knew when they were slumming in what they thought of as the Quarter and one would take me aside and talk to me seriously for my own good.   .

> "You mustn't let yourself go, Hem. It's none of my business, of course. But you can't go native this way. For God's sake straighten out and get a proper haircut at least."

> Then if I was ordered to some conference or to Germany or the Near East I would have to get a haircut and wear my one passable suit and my good English shoes and sooner or later I would meet the man who had straightened me out and he'd say,

> "You're looking fit old boy. Dropped that bohemian nonsense I see. What are you up to tonight? There's a very good place, absolutely special, up beyond Taxim's."

People who interfered in your life always did it for your own good and I
figured it out finally that what they wanted was for you to conform completely and never differ from some accepted surface standard and then dis-
sipate the way traveling salesmen would at a convention.[10]

This "goddamn newspaper stuff is gradually ruining me," Hemingway
wrote Sherwood Anderson as early as March 1922. He planned to "cut it all
loose pretty soon and work for about three months."[11] The *Toronto Star*
had other plans. First of all, John Bone wanted Hemingway to understand
that the overseas assignment was only temporary. "If when you return you
have a desire to live in Toronto," Bone emphasized on February 20, 1922,
"we shall be glad to find a place for you in the *Star* organization at a salary
of $75.00 a week." Six months later Bone reminded Hemingway that "if
you were here, both you and we would now be making even greater progress" as to money and career. Hemingway was disinclined to return, however. He was having a fine time traveling around Europe, cranking out feature material for the *Star* and crafting vignettes for himself. Greg Clark,
back in Toronto, could see Bone's point, but he sided with Hemingway.

It is the most natural thing in the world for Bone to want you home here.
He admits you have talent. I admit it. You admit it. It's unanimous. Therefore, why not use that talent, them gifts, every day of the week . . . instead of
being a desultory correspondent away abroad.
That is the way he sees it. He is building up a great staff.
But—I agree with you.
Why, at the age of twenty-four or five or whatever you are, should you pass
up the most wonderful education in the world to come back here to the drab
existence of even a star man on a second rate city paper?[12]

So the *Star* had their man in Europe for nearly all of 1922 and 1923, and
they took advantage of it. They sent Hemingway to Genoa for the economic
conference in April 1922; to the Near East for the Greco-Turkish fighting in
October 1922; to Lausanne for the Near East peace talks in November and
December 1922; to the occupied Ruhr in April and May 1923. They also
tried repeatedly to persuade Hemingway to go to Russia, sending him cre-
dentials and nudges from both Bone and Clark. "Your reputation is big
with us," Clark observed. "It will be bigger after Russia." For some reason—perhaps it was Hadley Hemingway, who did oppose Ernest's trip to
the embattled Near East—this proposition fell through.[13]

At the conferences, Hemingway widened his circle of influential acquaintances. He showed his fiction-in-progress to Max Eastman and Lincoln Staffens, and at Lausanne sat at the feet of the irreverent William
Bolitho Ryall, a South African who took his place alongside Moise in
Hemingway's journalistic pantheon. Ryall's distrust of power and of those
who wielded it only exacerbated Hemingway's debunking tendencies. Some
of his most successful dispatches, in fact, provided intimate glimpses of the

flaws in the physical and moral makeup of world leaders. Mussolini, Lloyd George, the Russian Tchitcherin—his stories reduced them all to human size. And the *Star* refused to print his interview with the one European leader he totally respected, Georges Clemenceau.

With Bill Bird of Consolidated Press, Hemingway went to interview Clemenceau at his seaside retreat in September 1922. The eleven page account he sent the *Star* typically stressed the physical appearance of the French leader:

> A bulky man, thickened by age, wearing a brown tweed suit, a funny, felt cap, his face as brown as an Ojibway, his white moustache drooping, his white eye-brows bushy, looking the tiger his pictures show him, his eyes twinkling as he talked to his plump daughter-in-law he came plodding through the sand.

The eyes were remarkable. "They are the only things you can see while you are talking to him. They seem to get inside of your eyes somehow and fasten claws there. When he is talking all his brown, healthy, chinese mandarin's face seems to have nothing to do with them."[14]

It was what Clemenceau said that made the interview unacceptable to the *Star*. Hemingway suggested that Clemenceau might visit Canada, but at the word Canada "his face went tiger." "I will *not* come to Canada," he responded, "emphasizing the not like an insult." The Canadians had "rejected compulsory service and refused to help France," he said. Never would he set foot there. The article went on to discuss the failure of the Versailles Treaty and the possibility that Clemenceau might yet return to power in France, but since the reference to Canada constituted the most interesting part of the article, John Bone did not think the paper should use it at all, "although"—he added to soften the blow—"I hate to pass up your excellent color to be found throughout the article."

In his letter of explanation, Bone was trying not to offend Hemingway and also to suggest where he had gone wrong. Bone did not bluntly insist, as Hemingway later maintained, that Clemenceau "can say these things, but he cannot say them in our paper." Instead he pointed out that the French leader was wrong about Canadian compulsory service, which was enacted and "in operation for a considerable period before the Armistice." Had Hemingway explained that point, perhaps the Tiger might have modified his statement. And if Clemenceau wanted to attack Canada, Bone went on, "all right, we can consider whether we will let him stir up bad feeling or not, but we should in no case allow him to do so in ignorance of facts which we ought to be in a position to give him."[15]

Actually, Hemingway was not in a good position to feel indignation toward the *Toronto Star*. On September 25, 1922, the very day that Bone posted his letter about Clemenceau, the *Star's* man in Europe entrained for Constantinople with a secret agreement to cable material to Frank Mason of

I.N.S. on the side, a clear violation of his exclusive contract with the *Star.* That double dealing "seared my Puritan soul," Hadley later remarked, and nobody felt entirely comfortable about the arrangement. Mason himself told Charles Fenton thirty years later that Hemingway contributed little of value to the wire service, and that he'd put the young correspondent on the expense account out of the kindness of his heart.[16] But that seems unlikely, since Hemingway sent enough copy to I.N.S. that it attracted the attention of John Bone back in Toronto.

The evidence suggests that Hemingway was sending the same Near East copy—or practically the same—both to the *Star* and to the wire service. That was true, for example, of one story on Kemal Pasha's single submarine in the Black Sea. The *Washington Times* of November 10, 1922, carried an article headed

Kemal's Lone Submarine Plays Pirate
in Black Seas as British
Hunt It

over the byline of "John Hadley, International News Service Staff Correspondent." On the same day, the *Toronto Daily Star* printed a Hemingway dispatch under the headline,

Destroyers Were on Lookout
For Kemal's One Submarine[17]

Hemingway and Mason probably felt they could get away with minimally rewritten copy since I.N.S. had no outlets in Canada. But somehow Bone got wind of I.N.S. material duplicating what he was paying for, and his query inspired Hemingway to a cock-and-bull explanation.

He's run low on funds in Constantinople, Hemingway told Bone, and thus cabled his stuff marked "Receiver to Pay" to Frank Mason of the International News Service in Paris, with instructions to relay it to the *Star's* London connection. Mason's office relayed it all right but also "proceeded to steal and re-write as much of it as they could get away with." He had placed more confidence in Mason's honesty than he should have done, Hemingway claimed, but he'd had it out with Mason now. "It was a personal matter and a question of ethics," he continued. Legally, Mason might have "a full right to re-write the dispatch considering the way it came to him, but ethically, as our ethics run in the profession over here, it was a very sorry business."[18]

The ethics became still sorrier several weeks later, when Hemingway—sent to Lausanne for the *Star*—surreptitiously signed on to supply additional reports not only to Mason at I.N.S. but also to the Universal News Service. This time, Hemingway avoided duplication of copy. He sent spot news to the wire services and saved the features for the *Star.* But there weren't many of the latter—Robert O. Stephens lists only two dispatches about Lausanne to the *Toronto Star,* and none before January, after the conference had ended—since covering the hard news amounted to a round-the-clock job. At that time, Hemingway later recalled, he "was running a twenty-four hour wire service for an afternoon and morning news service under two different names . . . ."

Not much is known about Hemingway's arrangements with the Universal News Service, except that Charles Bertelli—then the bureau chief in Paris—remembered hiring Hemingway to fill in for him at Lausanne. It may be that what Hemingway sent International News Service in Paris, under the John Hadley pseudonym, went automatically to Universal as well, since both agencies were owned by the Hearst organization. But the barrage of telegrams from Frank Mason to Hemingway betrays no awareness of this second news service connection. Probably Mason knew no more about Hemingway's arrangement with Universal than John Bone did about his agreement with I.N.S. The evidence, though not conclusive, suggests that the young correspondent may have been collecting expenses and/or salaries from as many as three different news organizations during the Near East peace talks in Lausanne.

The I.N.S. telegrams tell at least part of the story. Hemingway went on the wire service payroll on Wednesday, November 22, at a weekly rate of $60 for salary and expenses. That was hardly enough to pay for hotel living in Switzerland (customarily, the *Star* paid him after he'd completed his assignments, and we don't know about Universal), and Hemingway was stretched pretty thin, financially as well as physically. On November 27, he missed a news break: "new york cables tell hadley we scooped curzons open door announcement—mason." Instead of promising to do better, Hemingway wired back, "Story Broke 2230 oclock. Twenty four hour service costly." Mason chose to misunderstand: "ernest story was surely worth tolls don't understand whether costly refers tolls or what regards." It wasn't the telegraph tolls Hemingway had in mind, and Mason took steps to keep his man in Lausanne functioning: "ernest increase for expenses thirty-five dollars weekly beginning wednesday twentyninth inclusive confirmed stop carbons of your file look good regards."

In fact, however, Hemingway's next check came at the rate of $90 a week for salary and expenses instead of the agreed-upon $95. That kind of penny-pinching, it turned out, was characteristic of I.N.S. Mason kept reminding Hemingway to save his receipts for telegrams and other expenses in order to justify his pay. Finally, when Hemingway asked for 800 Swiss francs on December 14, Mason drew the line:

> ernest our books show approximately 500 swiss francs will be due you saturday but must have your receipts for continental telegrams and accounting for 250 originally advanced you before can make final settlement stop sending you our statement by mail express stop please rush your receipts and advise

balance due us stop advise whether you working inclusive saturday and saturday night kindest regards you both.

Hemingway shot back a response which capitalized on the possibilities for wit in the shorthand language of cablese:

INTERNEWS PARIS

SUGGEST YOU UPSTICK BOOKS ASSWARDS
HEMINGWAY

In a following letter he insisted that Mason's refusal to wire him the money had "smashed up" all his plans and caused him "a great deal of extra expense." He could only regard it as an unfriendly and insulting action. "There seems no possible way to regard your refusal to forward the money to me," Hemingway concluded, "except as a belief on your part that I was planning or trying to gyp you in some way."[19] Whatever could have caused Mason to think that?

Though the *Star* must have been disappointed by the paucity of Hemingway's Lausanne output, the paper nonetheless sent him off to the strife-ridden Ruhr for six weeks in the spring of 1923. Hemingway responded with some of his best articles, which combined sensitivity to the political and economic pressures which had led to French occupation of the area with characteristic attention to the human element, the effect of the occupation on the people he met and talked with. "I'm glad you liked the Franco-German articles," Ernest wrote his father in June. "They handle the show pretty well, at least make it an actual thing to people instead of simply a name on the map." John Bone liked them too, and ran six of Hemingway's articles on the front page of the *Daily Star*. All were by-lined, copyrighted; some, accompanied by house ads praising their reporter and his talents. "Hemingway has not only a genius for newspaper work, but for the short story as well," the *Star* proclaimed. "He is an extraordinarily gifted and picturesque writer. Besides his dispatches for the Star, he writes very little else, only two or three stories a year."[20]

In fact, his time on assignment in Switzerland and in the Ruhr earned him enough money so that he spent the summer polishing his fiction and, toward the end, preparing for the return to Toronto and the birth of John Hadley Nicanor Hemingway. When the *Andania* docked in Montreal August 27, there was a message from Bone welcoming him "home" and adding, in the patrician first person plural, "We shall be glad to see you in Toronto as soon as possible." Greg Clark, on the other hand, suggested that Hemingway rest up a week or so before reporting to the *Star*. The paper "needs you bad," Clark pointed out, "and you will be in a position to tear into things here and write your name in the skies."[21] Clark naturally assumed that the paper would want to capitalize on its investment in Hemingway as the star foreign correspondent in residence, but he failed to reckon with the tactics of Harry C. Hindmarsh, the *Daily Star's* assistant managing editor.

Hindmarsh, who was married to the daughter of the *Star's* publisher, was determined to rid the paper of any potential *prime donne*. He immediately decided that Hemingway needed his ego punctured and gave his new staffer a series of piddling assignments. He was awakened in the middle of the night to cover one-alarm fires. "Go over to city hall," he was told, "and see what's going on." For two weeks after he went on the payroll on September 10, nothing that Hemingway wrote was deemed worthy of a byline in the *Daily Star*,[22] a paper not at all stingy about bylines. Meanwhile, Hindmarsh was trying to convert his feature writer into an investigative reporter and Hemingway was busy with his homework.

He was directed to cover two different stories involving possible attempts to swindle the public, and at least one of these—the Sudbury coal rumor—Hemingway tackled with some enthusiasm. Back in Chicago, he had been placed in the uncomfortable position of writing inaccurate news releases in order to absolve his employers in the Co-operative Society of America of charges of wrongdoing. The society was not bankrupt at all, Hemingway had written on the basis of false information; the wife of the founder was on her way to Chicago with up to $3,000,000 in securities on her person.[23] The money never got there. Once bitten, twice shy.

On the basis of persistent reports that coal had been discovered in the Sudbury basin in Ontario, British Colonial Coal Mines Ltd. had begun selling shares of stock from an office in Toronto. By the time Hemingway took over the story, the *Star* had collected a dossier on one of the principals in the company, Alfred F. A. Coyne. Coyne, who had been involved in stock fraud charges in western Canada, presented himself as a petroleum geologist affiliated with the University of Manitoba. His only connection with that university, the *Star's* letter file revealed, was that he had once given a lecture to a geology club there, during which he made some extremely rash statements. "The only thing to do with Coyne," a University of Manitoba administrator advised, "is to cut off his head first and try him afterwards. If he were condemned to prison, he would in a week have the prison staff and all the inmates selling stock for some project of his."[24]

Four days after he officially began work for the *Star* in Toronto, Hemingway turned in a long and fascinating portrait involving two other principals in British Colonial Coal Mines Ltd., both of whom insisted that Coyne was no longer associated in their enterprise. Hemingway's account began by creating a climate of suspicion. "Although the British Colonial Coal Mines, Limited appears in the telephone directory as being located in the Temple Building they are not listed on the alphabetical list of Temple Building tenants posted in the corridor of the building." Behind a door on the eleventh floor marked "National Finance Company," Hemingway found Stewart Hood, president of British Colonial and J. W. Henderson, president of National Finance, the firm which sold shares in British Colonial. Impressionistically and satirically involving himself in the story as he had done with his dispatches from Europe, Hemingway chipped away at the credibility of these men. Hood, for example, took him through the following charade:

> Another man in a brown suit, a hawk face, his hair parted on the side and a little inclined to hang dankly forward at the parting [this was Hood], commenced talking. He had a charming voice. He started right out speaking very slowly and convincingly and smiling quizzically. "There's something here I want to show you," he said. "Here are two pieces of coal. Look them over." He handed them to me. They looked identical. They might have come from the same coal pile.
>
> "Look them over," the soft soothing voice urged. "Examine them carefully."
>
> I looked them over and examined them carefully. They looked like coal. The voice went on. The smile continued. There was the effect that it had all been said before. It was all so smooth, frank, reasonable and so straightforward.
>
> "One of those pieces of coal," the voice continued, "is from Pennsylvania. The other," he paused, "is from Sudbury." He smiled at me. Then in a smooth voice, accenting the word *which,* "Which is which?"
>
> Naturally I didn't know. But it was an even money shot so I picked. "This one came from Sudbury," I said.
>
> "That piece of coal," the voice purred on, "came from Pennsylvania." Somehow I felt it had.[25]

As Hemingway explained in a 12:30 a.m. memorandum to Hindmarsh, he had written out his story "in detail with the atmosphere and verbatim correspondence in case we get proof they are crooks and you decide to do an exposure." He wanted to get the copy down while it was still fresh in his head. There were no notes. "In a thing like this British Colonial it is impossible to make notes when you get them started contradicting etc. as the pencil would shut them right up," Hemingway explained, adopting the pose of expert.[26] Perhaps so, but the piece Hemingway submitted—though marvelously readable—was virtually unprintable. The *Star* did not run his copy. To do so would have invited a libel suit. What present-day journalists call the Afghanistan Principle was at work here. It was relatively safe to call Mussolini the biggest bluff in Europe or to poke fun at Tchitcherin's gaudy military uniform, but dangerous to say an unkind word about the local stock peddler.[27]

The *Star* editors still hoped to get to the bottom of the Sudbury case. Was there coal up there or not? So Hemingway went north with the rascally Coyne (who continued to hold stock in British Colonial and had also begun his own drilling operation nearby) and filed two rather dull stories on September 25 to the effect that there certainly was anthraxolite in the Sudbury

basin, but that drilling for coal remained a long shot. Two days later Coyne
sent Hemingway a ten-page typewritten report on the trip which the *Star*
was welcome to use "in part or whole." He only wanted to present his
"contentions . . . frankly," Coyne said, and was fully aware, as he dis-
ingenuously added, "that too rosy press reports in papers of the standing of
the *Star*, gives an opportunity for stock sellers to dupe the public." Some of
the fellows who'd gone along on the trip north, he couldn't help adding in a
postscript, had already put up money to keep the drilling going.[28] Needless
to say, the *Star* printed none of Coyne's self-interview and no more copy on
the subject from Hemingway either. When he had quit the *Star* and was on
his way back to Europe, Hemingway listed two "Stories to Write"—one
"The Story of the Sudbury Coal Co." and the other "The Son in Law," an
obvious reference to Harry C. Hindmarsh.[29]

His career as investigative reporter at an end, Hemingway was assigned to
any and all stories with a foreign flavor, from a Japanese earthquake to a
delegation from Hungary seeking a loan. When Lloyd George came to
North America early in October, Hemingway was sent to New York to report on his arrival. This would have been a desirable assignment but for two
things. First, Hemingway expected to have help from Mary Lowry and
Bobby Reade in covering the story, but in the end was asked to handle it by
himself. It was a big job: he filed two stories for October 5 and no fewer
than six for October 6. But he missed one solid news break, a speech by the
deputy mayor of New York containing ugly remarks about Great Britain.
Irate at being scooped, the *Star's* publisher ordered Hemingway off the
story, but he was already rushing home by then, since the second reason he
did not covet the Lloyd George assignment was that Hadley was about to
deliver. She had the baby early on the morning of October 10, when her
husband was still on the train north. Both she and Ernest blamed Hindmarsh for sending him away at such a crucial time.[30]

On October 11, Hindmarsh bawled Hemingway out at the office. He also
continued to send him memoranda full of elementary advice on how to handle stories, as if to the rawest of cub reporters. "I notice the *Globe* managed
to get a good interview with [Sir Henry] Thornton. I think we should have
stayed with him until we got him, as a personal interview yields a lot of
color in addition to subject matter." This to the paper's pre-eminent color
man! Then again, "I notice that Sir Henry Thornton is coming to Toronto
on November 5th . . . It is highly important that we secure a good article
from him this time and it would be advisable for you to start now to prepare
the subject and frame questions to put to him."[31]

If the assistant managing editor had set out to make Hemingway miser-
able, he could hardly have succeeded more effectively. Apparently, matters
came to a head a few days later in connection with Hemingway's interview
of Count Aponyi, a Hungarian diplomat. Aponyi gave Hemingway some

official documents to read, on condition that they be returned. Hemingway sent the documents to Hindmarsh asking him to place them in the office safe. Hindmarsh put them in the wastebasket instead and later in the day they were burned. That, at least, is the story that Hemingway told Cranston in 1951, and it is supported in part by the fact that Hemingway's story on the diplomatic mission, headed "Hungarian Statesman Delighted with Loan" and printed in the October 15 paper, was the last he wrote for the *Daily Star.*[32] After, that, he turned out copy for the *Star Weekly* supplement only, where he reported to Cranston and was somewhat less open to the carping of Hindmarsh.

Before he came to Toronto, he pointed out in a letter to John Bone, all his dealings had been with Bone. Since he joined the staff they had been with Mr. Hindmarsh, who had proved himself "neither a just man, a wise man, nor a very honest man." He had made every effort to get along with Hindmarsh, but it was no good. "I was horrified while handling a big story," Hemingway explained,

> . . . to be made the victim of an exhibition of wounded vanity from a man in a position of assistant managing editor on a newspaper of the caliber of the *Star* because he himself made a mistake. . . . For some reason Mr. Hindmarsh *says* that I think I know more about assignments he gives me than he does. I have given him no cause to think this and I cannot be accused of every [thing] that his inferiority complex suggests to him.

He realized that if it were a question of Hindmarsh or himself, he'd have to go, but, Hemingway concluded, it was "useless" for him "to continue to work on the *Star* under Mr. Hindmarsh."[33]

Immediately after the birth of their son, he and Hadley had begun making plans to return to Europe. The situation at the office, Hadley wrote a friend, "is too horrible to describe or linger over and it will kill or scar my Tiny if we stay too long."[34] Part of Hemingway's mind had already crossed the Atlantic. During the last months of 1923 he contributed features to the *Star Weekly* on bullfighting in Spain, hunting and fishing throughout the continent, Christmas in Paris, Christmas in Milan, night life in Constantinople. To seal the decision he sent Bone an official letter resigning "from the local staff of the *Star*" (thus leaving open the possibility of further foreign assignments) effective January 1, 1924. They'd planned to spend two years in Toronto, but the four months they spent there took five years off his life, Hemingway insisted. And he held Hindmarsh, "a son of a bitch and a liar," largely to blame.[35]

He'd never enjoyed himself so much, Hemingway told Cranston in 1951, as working with him and Greg Clark and Jimmy Frise. He'd been sad to quit newspaper work, but "working under Hindmarsh was like being in the

German army with a poor commander.'' After he'd become a famous fiction writer, Hemingway was asked to contribute to help organize a Newspaper Guild chapter at the *Star*. No union man himself, Hemingway first though of sending $100 "to beat Hindmarsh," then raised the ante. "On second thought I'm making it $200. I welcome the opportunity to take a swing at that ... Hindmarsh."[36]

You can still find would-be novelists languishing in the news rooms of every metropolitan daily in the country. Their work is not particularly onerous—they crank out news stories to a formula—but it takes time and after a while the good intentions peter out and no fiction gets written. Might Hemingway have suffered such a fate in a more congenial working environment than that of the *Toronto Star*? Probably not. Harry Hindmarsh helped drive him out of the newspaper business, but he doesn't deserve the entire credit, for Hemingway was different: he had more energy and ambition and talent than almost all of the news room yearners. From the beginning he knew he wanted to be a serious writer, and put journalism and fiction in two separate categories. He also got plenty of good advice from other writers about the dangers of over-exposure to the newspaper business. And significantly, in his own, mostly unpublished sketches about journalists, he tended to denigrate reporters and correspondents who did shoddy work and let their lives dwindle away.

As early as the Genoa conference in the spring of 1922, one of Hemingway's fellow foreign correspondents sensed that he "really didn't give a damn" about the job except as "it provided some much needed funds and gave him an association with other writers." Among those writers both Max Beerbohm and William Bolitho Ryall cautioned against the evils of tying oneself to commercial journalism. Gertrude Stein was still more eloquent on the subject. "You ruined me as a journalist last winter," Hemingway wrote her in the same letter that announced his decision to quit the *Star*. In their talks Stein told him "to get out of journalism and write as she said the one would use up the juice needed for the other." It was, Hemingway observed in 1951, "the best advice she ever gave me."[37]

Stein had warned that the reliance of newspaper writing upon presenting the facts might weaken one's inventive capacities and that its insistence upon timeliness might lead one to rely upon a false sense of immediacy. Hemingway was acutely conscious of both problems, particularly the second. The difference between "good writing" and "reporting," he observed in a 1935 *Esquire* article, was that no one would remember the reporting:

> When you describe something that has happened that day the timeliness makes people see it in their own imaginations. A month later that element of time is gone and your account would be flat and they would not see it in their minds nor remember it. But if you make it up instead of describing it you can make it round and whole and solid and give it life.[38]

Early and late, Hemingway insisted on his right not to be judged by his newspaper articles which had nothing to do with his serious writing. "If you have made your living as a newspaperman," he wrote Louis Henry Cohn prior to 1931, "learning your trade, writing against deadlines, writing to make stuff timely rather than permanent, no one has any right to dig this stuff up and use it against the stuff you have written to write the best you 'can." There are a few cases, as William White pointed out after quoting this letter, where Hemingway did little or nothing to his dispatches before printing them as stories.[39] In all other cases, however, Hemingway would have insisted on the distinction between journalism and fiction. Newspaper accounts distorted the facts by trivializing and sensationalizing experience, a point Hemingway made indirectly in a humorous piece on condensing the classics into journalistic jargon. Here are two samples:

CRAZED KNIGHT IN WEIRD TILT
Madrid, Spain—by Classic News Service—(Special)—

War hysteria is blamed for the queer actions of "Don" Quixote, a local knight who was arrested early yesterday morning when engaged in the act of "tilting" with a windmill. Quixote would give no explanation of his actions.

ALBATROSS SLAYER FLAYS PROHIBITION
Ancient Mariner in Bitter Assault/On Bone Dry Enforcement Cardiff, Wales, June 21. By Classic News Service (Delayed)—

"Water, water everywhere, and not a drop to drink" is the way John J. (Ancient) Mariner characterized the present prohibition regime in an address before the United Preparatory Schools here yesterday. Mariner was mobbed at the end of his address by a committee from the Ornithological Aid Society.[40]

The most remarkable thing about Hemingway's several portraits of other newspaper men is their lack of any sense of camaraderie. His satirical approach effectively distances Hemingway from his subjects. He is careful not to identify himself as one of the boys. While still working on the *Toronto Star*, for example, he pilloried one member of the staff for his "sodomistic leanings" and characterized another, his friend Greg Clark, with startling objectivity:

I have not done Greg justice. Maybe I have hurt him. It would be cruel to hurt him but also difficult because he is not flat but round all around. He would be hard to hurt because he is well rounded . . . He also loves to think. He thinks very well but never strains himself. He likes it about Canada too. What I dislike he dislikes too but it does not touch him. . . . You cannot dismiss him or classify him because he is always acting and you cannot tell how much of it is acting. He also acts inside himself. He is honestly interested in people. There is too much India rubber in him. I have never seen him angry. He has too much sense. If he has a weakness it is having too much sense.

Greg was his best friend on the paper, Hemingway wrote, but he did not really know him. He wished he'd seen Greg drunk and that he'd seen him cry. These were "the tests on a man."[41]

Far more drastically, Hemingway separated himself from the run-of-the mill war correspondent in several of his prose fragments. An introduction to his anti-war poems, "Champs d'Honneur" and "D'Annunzio," contrasts the writer's own authentic view of the war to the phony if supposedly patriotic one of some correspondents. They "wrote on their typewriters that a sergeant of marines said, 'Come on you sons of bitches do you want to live forever?' After which I suppose the men died gladly. But I saw tired soldiers burying dead soldiers and two of the tired ones carried one of the dead ones and they said, 'Jesus Christ this bastard's heavy.' "[42]

During the Spanish Civil War he encountered F. A. Voigt, a tall man with watery eyes who was covering the war for the *Manchester Guardian*, mostly from his hotel room. Voigt had just come to Madrid from Valencia.

"How does Madrid seem?" I asked him.

"There is a terror here," said Mr. Voigt. "There is evidence of it wherever you go. Thousands of bodies are being found."

"When did you get here?" I asked him.

"Last night."

"Where did you see the bodies?"

"They are around everywhere," he said. "You see them in the early morning."

"Did you see any bodies?"

"No," he said. "But I know they are there."

"What evidence of terror have you seen?"

"Oh it's there," he said. "You can't deny it's there."

"What evidence have you seen yourself?"

"I haven't had time to see it myself but I know it is there."

"Listen," I said. "You got in here last night. You haven't even been out in the town and you tell us who are living here and working here that there is a terror."

"You can't deny there is a terror," said Mr. Voigt. "Everywhere you see evidences of it."

"I thought you said you hadn't seen any evidences."

"They are everywhere," said Mr. Voigt.[43]

In yet another sketch Hemingway apparently set out to defame a World War II correspondent named Ed Rumson. The piece begins in praise of Rumson for his combat reporting. "I did not see how anyone could have seen so much fighting from so far forward without being hit or killed . . . and I thought Rumson must be one of those very lucky, unbelievably battle-wise characters who sizes up a situation instantly, who knows instinctively which side of a street you will be killed on and which you have a fair chance of staying alive on, and who has the luck to win all his even money bets."

The piece trails off before reaching the moment of disillusionment, but it is obviously on its way. When Hemingway meets Rumson in London, they become frequent companions. "I liked him in those days," Hemingway wrote, "because he was always good company" and because he was "almost always available," though "I did not know then why."[44]

Hemingway met few great reporters on the front lines, or if he did he did not choose to celebrate them. If anything he felt rather more sympathy for the burnt-out newpapermen who'd hung around the business too long. Hemingway made one such veteran reporter the hero of what may be his sole attempt at writing a murder mystery.

Morrow Alford, the newspaperman/detective of Hemingway's unpublished story, does not fit the media stereotype of the reporter. He doesn't look or talk hard-boiled. He doesn't have an intent piercing look or carry a great sheaf of copy paper. He is not writing a play that will make him famous in the last reel. He doesn't even smoke cigarettes. In fact Alford leads a dull everyday life. Every day he eats a roast beef sandwich and a glass of milk for lunch. Every evening he takes the 5:45 home to his wife, his kids, and his garden. The city editor calls him Punk. Alford is clever enough to figure out whodunit, but he's never going to amount to anything. "After fifteen years on the Gazette, Morrow Alford wished he had left the newpaper game in time, realized that it was too late, covered city politics for the day side, gardened in the evenings in the summer, studied seed catalogues in the winter and planned murder mystery stories that he started and never finished."[45]

Implicit in Hemingway's depiction of Punk Alford is the recognition that the "newspaper game" takes its toll on reporters. Elsewhere he made the point more explicitly. "In newspaper work," he observed in 1952, "you have to learn to forget every day what happened the day before." It was valuable experience "up to the point that it forcibly begins to destroy your memory. A writer must leave it before that point."[46] In a typescript fragment in the Kennedy Library, Hemingway compared "the real reporter" to a photographic plate:

> . . . when exposed to a murder, hanging, riot, great fire, eternal triangle or heavyweight box fight he automatically registers an impression that will be conveyed through his typewriter to the people who buy the paper. Great feature men are constructed like color photographing plates—humorous writers are cameras with a crooked, comically distorting lens. When a reporter ceases to register when exposed, he goes on the copy desk. There he edits the work of other men who haven't yet been exposed so many times as to cease to register.[47]

Hemingway of the *Star* was a first-rate feature man, with a comic bent that slightly distorted his color material. Unlike Punk Alford and many another reporter, he got out of newspaper work before too many exposures obliterated his memory and dulled his emotional capacity to react. It was a good thing for him, and for the rest of us.

NOTES

1 Philip Young, foreward to *Byline: Ernest Hemingway*, ed. William White (Harmondsworth: Penguin, 1970), p. 17.

2 Among the reviews of *Byline* which stressed the personal quality of Hemingway's journalism were Bernard Oldsey, "Always Personal," *Journal of General Education*, 19 (October 1967), 239-243, and William Kennedy, "The 'Clear Heart' of Reporter Hemingway," *National Observer* (29 May 1967), p. 19. It is somewhat ironical that in moving from journalism to fiction Hemingway had to reverse the usual procedure. That is, he had to remove from his fiction the self as commentator and ironist and expert which he had presented to readers of his newspaper work.

3 Some of the early *Toronto Star* dispatches from Europe were intimately related to stories, and even novels, that Hemingway later published. Two dissertations have focused on the process by which these journalistic pieces were transformed into fiction: Jasper Fred Kobler, III, "Journalist and Artist: The Dual Role of Ernest Hemingway," University of Texas dissertation, 1968, and John Alexander Shtogren, Jr., "Ernest Hemingway's Aesthetic Use of Journalism in His First Decade of Fiction," University of Michigan dissertation, 1971. Others who have explored this transformation with reference to specific articles and stories include Charles A. Fenton in *The Apprenticeship of Ernest Hemingway: The Early Years* (New York: Viking, 1958), pp. 229-236, and Malcolm Cowley in *A Second Flowering* (New York: Viking, 1973), pp. 64-66 (both on the Thracian retreat). Fenton's book remains an invaluable source for anyone interested in Hemingway's newspaper career.

4 For what Hemingway learned on the *Kansas City Star*, see Fenton, pp. 28-49. The Moise reminiscence constitutes Item 553 of the Hemingway Collection in the John F. Kennedy Library. For her considerable assistance in the preparation of this paper and her instinctive understanding of what it is that scholars are looking for, I am indebted like many others to Jo August, curator of the Hemingway Collection.

5 For discussion of Hemingway's satirical tendencies, see Fenton, pp. 81, 86-87, 110-113.

6 Ernest Hemingway (EH) to John R. Bone, 2 March 1921, and Gregory Clark to EH, 28 February 1921 and 13 April 1921, Hemingway Collection.

7 EH to John R. Bone, 26 October 1921, Hemingway Collection. This letter (or draft of a letter?) trails off without concluding.

8 Carlos Baker, *Ernest Hemingway: A Life Story* (New York: Scribner's, 1969), p. 82; Fenton, pp. 115-116.

9 Fenton, p. 119.

10 Item 256, Hemingway Collection. Hemingway may have contemplated using this manuscript as part of *A Moveable Feast*; it has much the same tone and attitude as, for example, the discussion of the rich in that book. The manuscript is written in pencil with an inked heading, "Worthless Sketch Discarded." The be-

ginning, reproduced above, is much the best part of the piece, which goes on to a long celebration of hair in general and Hadley's hair in particular.

11 EH to Sherwood Anderson, 9 March 1922, Hemingway Collection.

12 John R. Bone to EH, 20 February 1922 and 20 August 1922, and Gregory Clark to EH, 21 November 1922, Hemingway Collection.

13 John R. Bone to EH, 8 April 1922, and Gregory Clark to EH, 2 September 1922, Hemingway Collection. Also see Baker, p. 578. In a cable to Bone dated 9 May (1922 or 1923?), Hemingway declined to take the trip:
RUSSIA UNFEASIBLE FOR ME AT PRESENT UNLESS
EMERGENCY STOP LETTER FOLLOWING HEMINGWAY

14 Item 773b (in part), Hemingway Collection.

15 John R. Bone to EH, 25 September 1923, Hemingway Collection. Hemingway construed Bone to mean that "Clemenceau can say these things, but he cannot say them in our paper" in "a.d. Southern Style," *Esquire*, 3 May (1935), 25.

16 Baker, p. 97; Scott Donaldson, *By Force of Will: The Life and Art of Ernest Hemingway* (New York: Viking, 1977), p. 38; Fenton, pp. 171, 281.

17 Clipping from the *Washington Times*, 10 November 1922, Hemingway Collection; list of Hemingway's non-fiction articles in Robert O. Stephens, *Hemingway's Nonfiction: The Public Voice* (Chapel Hill: University of North Carolina Press, 1968), p. 352.

18 EH to John R. Bone, 27 October 1922, Hemingway Collection; Baker, p. 579.

19 Stephens, p. 352; EH, "The Malady of Power," *Byline*, p. 215; Fenton, pp. 188-189; telegrams and letters from Frank Mason or the I.N.S. Paris office to EH, 24 November 1922, 25 November 1922, 27 November 1922, 28 November 1922 (twice), 29 November 1922, 4 December 1922, 14 December 1922, 15 December 1922; EH to Frank Mason, 14 (?) December 1922 and 15 December 1922, Hemingway Collection.

20 EH to Dr. C. E. Hemingway, 20 June 1923, Hemingway Collection; Fenton, pp. 222-223.

21 John R. Bone to EH, 18 August 1923, and Gregory Clark to EH, 31 August 1923, Hemingway Collection.

22 For a further description of Hindmarsh's reputation and method of operation, see Fenton, pp. 244-246.

23 Items 576 and 722, Hemingway Collection; Fenton, pp. 96-99.

24 The file on Coyne is in Item 682b, Hemingway Collection.

25 Hemingway's report on British Colonial Coal Mines, Ltd., along with a letter to Hindmarsh, constitutes part of Item 682a, Hemingway Collection. The report is dated 14 September 1923.

26 Item 682c, Hemingway Collection.

27 Hemingway's first article for the the Toronto papers after his return to Canada, which appeared on page one of the *Star Weekly* for 15 September 1923, humorously treated the subject of current European royalty. The characterization of King Alexander of Serbia drew an irate letter from A. Papineau Mathieu demanding a denial. Nothing much came of this demand, since Hemingway was apparently on safe ground in suggesting that the monarch preferred Parisian night life to the duties of state. "Various girls were at his table," the *Star Week-*

ly story observed. "It was a big night for the wine growers. Alexander was quite drunk and very happy."

28 Item 682b, Hemingway Collection, includes a memo from Bone asking point blank, "Is there coal in the Sudbury district?"

29 Hemingway listed the Sudbury story as one to write in Items 386 and 720a, Hemingway Collection.

30 Fenton, p. 289; Stephens, pp. 352-353; Baker, pp. 116-117.

31 Item 773e and notes from Harry C. Hindmarsh to EH, Hemingway Collection.

32 Fenton, p. 256; Stephens, p. 353.

33 EH to John R. Bone, undated, Hemingway Collection. This is a draft.

34 Baker, p. 117.

35 For titles of articles on Europe, see Stephens, pp. 353-354. EH to John R. Bone, letter of resignation, n.d., and Item 274a, Hemingway Collection; Fenton, pp. 243, 261.

36 Fenton, pp. 256-257.

37 Fenton, pp. 138, 158-159, 194; Baker, p. 89; EH to Gertrude Stein and Alice B. Toklas, 9 November 1923, Hemingway Collection.

38 Fenton, pp. 158-159; EH, "Monologue to the Maestro," *Byline*, pp. 208-209.

39 William White quotes Hemingway's letter to Louis Henry Cohn on this subject in *Byline*, p. 13.

40 Item 335, Hemingway Collection. This appeared as "Condensing the Classics," *Toronto Star Weekly* (20 August 1921), p. 22.

41 Item 247a, Hemingway Collection.

42 Items 326 and 326a, Hemingway Collection.

43 Item 411, Hemingway Collection.

44 Item 481, Hemingway Collection.

45 Item 581, Hemingway Collection.

46 Quoted in Fenton, p. 161.

47 Item 270.5, Hemingway Collection.

HEMINGWAY'S LIBRARY:
SOME VOLUMES OF POETRY

James D. Brasch and Joseph Sigman

In his edition of *88 Poems* by Ernest Hemingway, Nicholas Gerogiannis notes that although Hemingway, like Joyce, Faulkner, and Fitzgerald, "composed a certain amount of verse while he was becoming an established fiction writer," he also "continued to experiment with poetry after he had achieved literary fame."[1] Hemingway's interest in poetry was not limited, however, to writing a small amount of verse at various times. He was also throughout his life a reader of poetry. Our complete bibliography of Hemingway's library, which will be published by Garland Press in 1981, lists 229 volumes of poetry. Hemingway read poetry in French, Spanish, and Italian as well as in English, and the poetry volumes in his library are remarkably diverse, ranging from W. H. Auden's *Oxford Book of Light Verse* and Robert Bridge's edition of the poems of Gerard Manley Hopkins to Lamartine's *Meditations poétique* and including exotic items such as a Spanish translation of Shelley's *Adonais*. In the present essay, we will focus primarily on four poets, two from the 20th Century and two from the 19th Century, in whom, it is clear, Hemingway maintained a serious interest over a long period of time, but we will also glance at a number of related figures.

Hemingway's admiration for Ezra Pound is well-known, and it is not surprising, therefore, that there are more volumes by Pound in Hemingway's library than by any other poet. These volumes range chronologically from a 1916 *Gaudier-Brzeska* to a 1958 *Pavannes and Divagations*; so it is clear that Hemingway's interest in the work of his old mentor never waned. The following is a complete list of the volumes of Pound's poetry in Hemingway's possession:

A lume spento, 1908-1958. A cura di Vanni Scheiwiller. Milan: Antonini, 1958.

Cantos 91, 96. Brani tradotti da Enzo Siciliano. Genoa, 1958.

A Draft of XVI Cantos of Ezra Pound for the Beginning of a Poem of Some Length. Now first made into a book with initials by Henry Strater. Paris: Three Mountains, 1925.

A Draft of XXX Cantos. New York: Farrar & Rinehart, 1933.

Lustra. [Edition unknown.][2]

Personae: The Collected Poems, Including Ripostes, Lustra, Homage to Sextus Propertius, H. S. Mauberley. New York: Boni & Liveright, 1926.

Selected Poems. Edited with an introduction by T. S. Eliot. London: Faber & Gwyer, 1928.

The Translations of Ezra Pound. Introduction by Hugh Kenner. New York: New Directions, n.d.

Umbra: The Early Poems of Ezra Pound, All that He Now Wishes to Keep in Circulation from "Personae", Exultations", Ripostes", etc. With translations from Guido Cavalcanti and Arnaut Daniel, and poems by the late T. E. Hulme. London: Elkin Mathews, 1920.

In addition to these volumes, Hemingway owned the following anthology, which contains six poems by Pound as well as poems by other modernists such as Joyce, Williams, MacLeish, and Hemingway himself:

Profile: An Anthology Collected in MCMXXXII. Milan: Ferrari, 1932.

Hemingway also owned nine volumes of Pound's prose:

A B C of Economics. [Edition unknown.]

A B C of Reading. Norfolk, Conn.: New Directions, n.d.

Antheil and the Treatise on Harmony. Paris: Three Mountains, 1924.

Gaudier-Brzeska: A Memoir. London: Lane, 1916.

Guide to Kulchur. London: Faber, 1938. [Two copies.]

Lavoro ed usura: Tre saggi. Milan: All'Insegna del Pesce d'Oro, 1954.

Make It New: Essays. [Edition unknown.]

Pavannes and Divagations. Norfolk, Conn.: New Directions, 1958. [Two copies.]

Pavannes and Divisions. [Edition unknown.]

Hemingway acquired two copies of D. D. Paige's edition of *The Letters of Ezra Pound, 1907-1941*, which was published in 1950 by Harcourt, Brace.

The other 20th Century poet whose career Hemingway followed with considerable attention was T. S. Eliot. Once again, the volumes were acquired over a long period of time, and there are volumes of literary and social criticism as well as poetry. Although Hemingway certainly knew of Eliot's work when he was in Paris in the 1920's, the earliest surviving Eliot volume in the library is a 1929 Faber edition of *Dante*. This volume has a sticker in the back that indicates that it was purchased at Shakespeare and Co. in Paris. Probably, therefore, Hemingway acquired it during his visit to Paris in 1931. His interest in Eliot was still active over twenty years later, when he acquired a copy of *The Complete Poems and Plays*. The following is a complete list of the titles by Eliot in Hemingway's library:

After Strange Gods: A Primer of Modern Heresy. [Edition unknown.]

The Cocktail Party. New York: Harcourt, Brace, 1950.

Collected Poems, 1909-1935. New York: Harcourt, Brace, 1936.

The Complete Poems and Plays. New York: Harcourt, Brace, 1952.

Dante. London: Faber, 1929.

From Poe to Valery. New York: Harcourt, Brace, 1948.

Murder in the Cathedral. [Edition unknown.]

Poems, 1909-1925. London: Faber, 1933.

Selected Essays. [Edition unknown.]

The Use of Poetry and the Use of Criticism: Studies in the Relation of Criticism to Poetry in England. London: Faber, 1933.

There are as many volumes by Archibald MacLeish in Hemingway's library as by Eliot, but in general there is not the same impression of intense interest conveyed by the three collected editions of Eliot's poems. We have no evidence that Hemingway acquired the collected edition of MacLeish's poetry published in 1953. Furthermore, MacLeish and Hemingway knew each other well and some, at least, of the MacLeish volumes were given to Hemingway by MacLeish as gifts. For example, the 1948 edition of *Actfive and Other Poems* is inscribed by MacLeish to Hemingway. The following are the volumes by MacLeish in Hemingway's Library:

Actfive and Other Poems. New York: Random House, 1948.

Air Raid: A Verse Play for Radio. [Edition unknown.]

America Was Promises. [Edition unknown.]

Conquistador. Boston: Houghton Mifflin, 1933.

The Hamlet of A. MacLeish. [Edition unknown.]

New Found Land: Fourteen Poems. [Edition unknown.]

Public Speech: Poems. [Edition unknown.]

Songs for Eve. Boston: Houghton Mifflin, 1954.

Streets in the Moon. Boston: Houghton Mifflin, 1926.

The Trojan Horse. Boston: Houghton Mifflin, 1952.

Various other 20th Century poets writing in English are represented by multiple volumes in the library, but in none of these cases does the diversity or chronological range of the volumes indicate a depth of involvement comparable to that demonstrated by the Pound and Eliot holdings. Three poets who do stand out, however, are W. H. Auden, William Butler Yeats, and Edna St. Vincent Millay. The volumes by Auden are:

Another Time: Poems. New York: Random House, 1940.

The Collected Poetry of W. H. Auden. New York: Random House, 1945.

Look, Stranger! London: Faber, 1936.

Poems. [Edition unknown.]

With Christopher Isherwood. *The Ascent of F6: A Tragedy in Two Acts*. London: Faber, 1937.

With Christopher Isherwood. *The Dog Beneath the Skin; or, Where is Francis? A Play in Three Acts*. London: Faber, 1935.

The volumes by Yeats are:

Autobiographies: Reveries over Childhood and Youth and The Trembling of the Veil. [Edition unknown.]

Collected Poems. Definitive edition with the author's final revisions. New York: Macmillan, 1957.

Dramatis Personae, 1896-1902, Estrangement, The Death of Synge, The Bounty of Sweden. New York: Macmillan, 1936.

Later Poems. New York: Macmillan, 1924.

Poems. [Edition unknown.]

The volumes by Millay are:

Collected Sonnets. New York: Harper, 1941.

Letters. Edited by Allan Ross Macdougall. New York: Harper, 1952.

Poems. [Edition unknown.]

Poems Selected for Young People. New York: Harper, 1929.

Second April. [Edition unknown.]

Hemingway also owned five volumes by William Carlos Williams, but he was clearly more interested in Williams' prose than in his poetry:

Autobiography. New York: Random House, 1951.

Life Along the Passaic River. [Edition unknown.]

Selected Poems. Introduction by Randall Jarrell. New York: New Directions, 1949.

A Voyage to Pagany. [Edition unknown.]

White Mule. [Edition unknown.]

Two additional 20th Century poets writing in English are represented in the library by four volumes. These are Marianne Moore and E. E. Cummings. In the case of Marianne Moore, Hemingway's interest was long-lasting and included the purchase of the collected edition of her poems published in 1951:

Collected Poems. New York: Macmillan, 1951.

Marriage. New York: Wheeler, 1923.

Predilections. New York, Vikings, 1955.

Selected Poems. Introduction by T. S. Eliot. New York: Macmillan, 1935.

In the case of Cummings, the book that appears to have most impressed him was *The Enormous Room*. The volumes by Cummings in the library are:

Eimi. New York: Covici, Friede, 1933.

The Enormous Room. With an introduction by the Author. New York: Modern Library, 1922.

Is 5. New York: Boni & Liveright, 1926.

1 x 1. New York: Holt, 1944.

When one turns to the 19th Century poets with whom Hemingway was most seriously involved, Charles Baudelaire and Lord Byron, the early publication dates of some of the volumes of their works in Hemingway's possession make it difficult to ascertain when he first read their works. Other information is available, however, which makes it clear that Hemingway was involved with their work over a considerable span of time. It seems likely that he first encountered Baudelaire's works in Paris during the 1920's. It is highly probable that when he lived in Key West in the 1930's he owned a copy of Baudelaire's *Intimate Journals*, translated by Christopher Isherwood, with an introduction by T. S. Eliot. In 1941, a copy of *Les fleurs du mal et complément* was moved from Key West to Cuba. Some time after his return from Europe in 1945, Hemingway acquired a copy of Edwin Morgan's *Flower of Evil: A Life of Charles Baudelaire*, which had been published in 1943 by Sheed & Ward. Finally, in 1948 Hemingway gave Mary Hemingway a copy of *Les fleurs du mal*, with illustrations by Rodin, which he dedicated to her in French. This is a complete list of the volumes by Baudelaire in the library:

Les fleurs du mal. Précedées d'une notice par Theophile Gautier. Paris: C. Lévy, 1894.

Les fleurs du mal. Illustrées par Auguste Rodin avec une préface de Camille Mauclair. Paris: The Limited Editions Club, 1940.

Les fleurs du mal et complément. [Edition unknown.]

Les fleurs du mal. Stockholm: Jan Förlag, 1944.

Intimate Journals. Translated by Christopher Isherwood. [Introduction by T. S. Eliot? Edition unknown.]

Morceaux chosis: Poëmes et proses. Introduction et notes par Y. G. Le Dantec. Paris: Gallimard, 1939.

Two other French poets, younger contemporaries of Baudelaire, also seem to have interested Hemingway. A letter to Richard L. Nelson on Sept. 9, 1949, mentions receiving from him copies of "Verline" and Rimbaud. Two volumes by Paul Verlaine are in the library:

Oeuvres posthumes. Vol. 3: Vers inédits. Critique et conferences. Appendice. Paris: Messein, 1929.

Poèmes saturniens. [Edition unknown, but among books moved to Cuba in 1941.]

Only one volume by Arthur Rimbaud has survived in the library:

Lettres de la vie littéraire. [Edition unknown.]

In the case of Lord Byron, there can be no doubt that at least by the 1930's Hemingway was fascinated by the Englishman's life—more so, perhaps, than by his poetry. A 1933 Dent edition of Byron's letters was moved from Key West to Cuba in 1941. In addition, that same shipment contained three biographies of Byron: those by Peter Quennell, Harold Nicolson, and André Maurois. It is equally clear that this fascination never waned, for in 1957 Hemingway acquired a copy of Leslie Marchand's three-volume life of Byron. The following are the works by Byron in Hemingway's library:

Byron, A Self-portrait: Letters and Diaries, 1798 to 1824, with Hitherto Unpublished Letters. Edited by Peter Quennell. New York: Scribner, 1950.

Child Harold's Pilgrimage. [Edition unknown.]

The Complete Poetical Works. Boston: Houghton Mifflin, 1905.

Don Juan: A Satirical Epic of Modern Life. New York: Heritage, 1943.

His Very Self and Voice: Collected Conversations. Edited by Ernest J. Lovell, Jr. New York: Macmillan, 1954.

The Letters of George Gordon, 6th Lord Byron. Selected by R. G. Howarth with an introduction by André Maurois. London: Dent, 1933.

The Life, Letters and Journals of Lord Byron. [Edition unknown.]

Poetical Works. [Edition unknown.]

Seven biographies of Byron are also in the library:

Quennell, Peter. *Byron: The Years of Fame.* New York: Viking, 1935.

Quennell, Peter. *Byron in Italy.* New York: Viking, 1941.

Origo, Iris. *The Last Attachment: The Story of Byron and Teresa Guiccioli As Told in Their Unpublished Letters and Other Family Papers.* New York: Scribner, 1949.

Nicolson, Harold George. *Byron: The Last Journey.* London: Constable, 1934.

Mayne, Ethel Colburn. *Byron.* [Edition unknown.]

Maurois, André. *Byron.* 2 vols. [Edition unknown.]

Marchand, Leslie A. *Byron: A Biography.* 3 vols. New York: Knopf, 1957.

Hemingway owned copies of the works of many of the standard English and American poets. The following volumes, for example, are in his library:

The Complete Poetry and Selected Prose of John Donne and The Complete Poetry of William Blake in One Volume. New York: Random House, 1941.

The Poetical Works of John Keats. [Edition unknown.]

Alexander Pope. *Complete Poetical Works.* Boston: Houghton Mifflin, 1903.

The Poetical Works of John Milton. New York: Burt, n.d.

Dante Gabriel Rossetti. *The Poetical Works.* New York: Crowell, n.d.

Percy Bysshe Shelley. *Selected Poetry and Prose*. Edited with an introduction by Carlos Baker. New York: Modern Library, 1951.

William Wordsworth. *The Prelude; with a Selection from the Shorter Poems*. [Edited by Carlos Baker. New York: Rinehart?]

Emily Dickinson. *Poems*. Boston: Little, Brown, 1952.

Walt Whitman. *Leaves of Grass*. [Edition unknown.]

Walt Whitman. *Poems and Prose*. [Edition unknown.]

In closing, it is appropriate to mention a work that appears to have had some special significance to Hemingway. This is Shakespeare's *Sonnets*. In Mary Hemingway's personal library there is an edition of the sonnets, edited by M. R. Ridley and published in London by Dent in 1938. The volume is signed by Hemingway with the note "Re-read Kenya 1957." Mary Hemingway has remarked on several occasions that she often read poetry to Hemingway at night and that *The Sonnets* was one of the volumes she would sometimes read. In her autobiography, *How It Was*, she gives this account of reading to Hemingway when he was ill with hepatitis in the mid-1950's:

> I bought a reading lamp to put behind the chair at the foot of his bed and many evenings read aloud all sorts of people, from Shakespeare (the sonnets) to T. E. Lawrence to Jim Corbett to Anne Morrow Lindbergh to *The Oxford Book of English Verse*. [3]

In addition to the Dent edition of the sonnets and a number of complete works of Shakespeare that included the sonnets, there are in the library two translations of the sonnets into Italian:

Sonetti. Introduzione e traduzione di Alberto Rossi. Turin: Einaudi, 1952.

Giuseppe Ungaretti, tr. *Tradusioni*. [40 sonetti di Shakespeare. Da Góngora e da Mallarmé. Fedra di Jean Racine. Visioni di William Blake.] Milan: Mondadori, 1946.

NOTES

1 Ernest Hemingway, *88 Poems*, ed. with intro. by Nicholas Gerogiannis (New York, 1979), p. xi.

2 "Edition unknown" indicates that our source did not record details of publication. For a complete description of all of our sources see our forthcoming volume.

3 Mary Hemingway, *How It Was* (New York, 1976), p. 428.

THE MYSTERY OF THE RITZ HOTEL PAPERS

Jacqueline Tavernier-Courbin

As we all know, *A Moveable Feast* is a series of reminiscences written by Hemingway during the last years of his life about the years he spent in Paris with his first wife, Hadley, between 1922 and 1926. Much has been made of the fact that, in November 1956, Hemingway supposedly retrieved from the basement of the Ritz Hotel in Paris two trunks which he had left there in 1927. Mary Hemingway, the writer's last wife, and apparently Hemingway himself claimed that it was the discovery of the old papers and manuscripts contained in those trunks that gave him the idea of writing his memoirs of the old days in Paris, and that he used that material of thirty years past in the composition of the book.

This is a very nice story, very much in the same vein as that of the discovery of James Boswell's journals, and there seems to be little reason to doubt it. However, the various accounts of the discovery are often conflicting, and, so far, I have not found a direct statement by Hemingway himself concerning the discovery of the trunks. Moreover, he is reported to have claimed that he found in these trunks manuscripts which could not, in fact, have been there. It is, therefore, important to attempt to determine three things: 1) whether these trunks really existed and, if so, at what time they were left at the Ritz; 2) what papers were in them; and 3) what use Hemingway made of these papers in the writing of *A Moveable Feast*.

There were various reports concerning the discovery of the trunks even before Mary Hemingway's description of them in the *New York Times Book Review* of May 10, 1964. In fact, the story seems to have originated with Leonard Lyons who, in his column "The Lyons Den" of December 11, 1957, mentions the discovery and reports that Hemingway told him that the manuscript of *A Farewell to Arms* was in the trunks, which could hardly have been the case since Hemingway had given that manuscript to Gus Pfeiffer in 1930. Lyons mentions again the discovery of the trunks in his column of December 9, 1963, after Mary Hemingway's press-conference. However, it seems that Mary Hemingway had not talked about that discovery in her press-conference since none of the other responses to it refer to the trunks. The story came out in force in April 1964 with the review of George P. Hunt in *Life* and, on May 10, with both Mary Hemingway's and Lewis Galantière's in *The New York Times Book Review*, Mildred Carr's in the *Greensborro Daily News* and Reece Stuart's in *The Des Moines Register*.[1] Mary Hemingway describes the trunks as follows:

They were two small, fabric-covered, rectangular boxes, both opening at the seams . . . . The baggage men easily pried open the rusted locks, and Ernest was confronted with the blue-and-yellow-covered penciled notebooks and sheaves of typed papers, ancient newspaper cuttings, bad water colors done by old friends, a few cracked and faded books, some musty sweat shirts and withered sandals. *Ernest had not seen the stuff since 1927, when he packed it and left it at the hotel before going to Key West.* (Italics added.)

Mildred Carr is very cautious and, although she gives various details concerning the composition of the book, which she probably obtained from Mary Hemingway or from Hadley—such as the fact that Hemingway telephoned Hadley to ask her to refresh his memory about certain people—she begins her mention of the trunks with "It is said that." Other less careful reviewers used their imagination to fill in the details and even transformed the notebooks contained in the trunks into diaries.

At this point, I should like to make two comments on Mary Hemingway's description of the event. First, she mentions that Ernest had left these trunks at the Ritz in 1927 before going to Key West, which is clearly an error since he did not go to Key West until late March 1928.[2] Similarly, elsewhere in her article, she indicates that the baggage men at the Ritz had asked Hemingway to remove his trunks since 1936, when he had been on his way home from Spain. Again, it is not until May 9 to 13, 1937, that Hemingway was in Paris on his way home from Spain. Mary Hemingway's own report, therefore, contains some inaccuracies.

Of course, after the so-called description of the Ritz-Hotel papers by Mary Hemingway and other early reviewers, many scholars and critics described these papers with some assurance and assumed their importance for the composition of *A Moveable Feast*. What is important is not only the fact that everyone took the existence of the trunks and the papers for granted but also the fact that it has been widely held that Hemingway had written the better parts of *A Moveable Feast* in the early Twenties and the rest—the inferior parts—before his death. Some have even believed that the whole book was written in the Twenties. In fact, the purported use of the old manuscripts discovered in the trunks in the writing of the book has often been seen as evidence that Hemingway had lost his talent and was reduced to plagiarizing his past. That Hemingway found it very hard to write in 1960 and 1961 has been well documented. But, as we shall see, although Hemingway did indeed use some of his earlier writings in the book, he used far less than one might imagine.

A. E. Hotchner's account of his last visit to Hemingway in 1961 enhanced the theory that Hemingway had written the book earlier. Hotchner quotes Hemingway as saying, "The best of that (*A Moveable Feast*) I wrote before. And now I can't finish it."[3] What Hemingway probably meant is that he had written the book in 1956-1957. Indeed, he had considered it as finished in 1960 when he sent it to Scribner's. He withdrew the manuscript, however, for at least two reasons: officially, because he wanted to improve it (as evidenced by his letter to Charles Scribner of March 31, 1960), but also, probably, because he was afraid of libel suits, as shown by the many drafts he wrote of the preface to the book.

It is interesting to notice that what probably started out as inaccurate reporting on Lyon's part, or even as a distortion of the truth on Hemingway's part, became an accepted fact after Mary Hemingway's review of the book and was generally seen as Hemingway's major motivation for writing his memoirs. Interestingly, Mary Hemingway contradicts herself somewhat in her later description of the event in *How It Was*.[4] It is not necessary to quote at length, but the details that she gives concerning the discovery of the trunks are quite different from the details of her earlier account. The progression in her accounts from a rather casual incident to a much more formal occurence reflects the increasing importance given with time to those trunks and their manuscript contents for the composition of *A Moveable Feast*.

The evidence supporting the fact that Hemingway had left trunks of old manuscripts in Paris—if not necessarily at the Ritz—in the last 1920s, apart from Mary Hemingway's claim, and the evidence which suggests that the discovery of the Ritz-Hotel papers was part of Hemingway's myth-making are almost evenly balanced.

Apart from Hemingway's reported claim, and Mary's direct claim, that he found two trunks of old manuscripts in the basement of the Ritz, there are in Hemingway's correspondence various references to old papers, manuscripts and letters stored in Paris. Probably the most reliable piece of evidence to that effect is to be found in a letter from Hemingway to Gus Pfeiffer dated March 16, 1928. Gus had asked Hemingway for the manuscripts of "Fifty Grand" and "The Undefeated," and Hemingway wrote back to him:

> I have hunted through all my old trunks here at the apartment to find the manuscripts of Fifty Grand and The Undefeated so I could send them to you. But have found 8 or 10 other mss. but not those. Evidently they are in storage with my 4 trunks of old letters and mss.
>
> So I am enclosing the manuscript of The Killers, the first typescript of The Undefeated and the only part I have found of Fifty Grand. The part I eliminated in publishing it. I hope you will hold these as hostages—they are for you too—until I can find the manuscripts you want when we return in the fall. I put in 6 hours or so going through old stuff in order to "make delivery" but havent [sic] found them yet (I never placed any value on them and so did not keep. . . track of them in all my very varied stuff) and am sure they are in storage.[5]

Hemingway was by that time already very fond of Gus Pfeiffer, who had been very good to him and Pauline, and there seems to be no reason why he should lie to him. "When we return in the fall" has to mean "when we return to Paris" for Hemingway had not yet settled in Key West, and the apartment he refers to is the Rue-Férou apartment. However, he mentions four trunks and not two, and certainly makes no mention of the Ritz Hotel. Although the date of this letter coincides closely with the time at which Hemingway is supposed to have left his trunks at the Ritz, it does not seem, by the contents of it, that he was doing any such thing.

In a letter to Julien Cornell concerning the release from prison of Ezra Pound, Hemingway writes on December 11, 1945:

> I do not have any of Ezra Pound's letters here, since I do not believe he has written me since 1935 or 1936. It is very probable that I have some of his old letters stored in Paris.

However, in a hand-written draft of that same letter, he had added: "or, possibly in Key West." Again this suggests the possibility of papers stored in Paris, although there is no certainty that Pound's letters were among them. However, it may also be merely an excuse on Hemingway's part for not taking the trouble to search for Pound's letters in order to send them to Cornell. Pound's letter would, in fact, have added little fuel to Hemingway's claim that he was crazy.

A third and final, although least reliable, reference to papers stored in Paris can be found in a letter from Hemingway to Arnold Gingrich dated November 16, 1934, in which he writes:

> Like Seldes [Gilbert], I've had him worried about that letter for a very long time now and I'm going to keep him worried. Don't say I mentioned it anymore. I've got it locked up with my papers in Paris and no matter how his critical career comes out this makes a bum of him in the end. I've written all the facts about Gertrude so they'll be on tap if anything happens to me but I don't like to slam the old bitch around when she's here having a wonderful time.

This is probably mostly bluster, for I have not yet been able to locate any such letter from Gilbert Seldes, and Seldes himself strongly denies it.[6] Although there are several rather cruel references to Gertrude Stein among Hemingway's papers, there does not seem to be any manuscript such as the one he refers to here. The papers supposedly stored in Paris were a rather handy weapon for Hemingway, who seems to have had an obsession for claiming that he had concrete evidence to damn his contemporaries.

Thus, at various times in his life, Hemingway claimed that he had papers stored in Paris. However, not all of his old papers were stored there, as evidenced by the draft of his letter to Julien Cornell, as well as by a letter to Mizener, dated July 6, 1949, in which he claims that he had Fitzgerald's old letters in Key West for a time:

> I am very sorry that I do not have any of Scott's letters here. Most of them were stored in Key West and were probably eaten by mice and roaches . . . . I had everything filed in a cabinet and in pretty good order, but while I was away at one of the wars someone decided to use the cabinet to keep their files while setting up a small antique business and as a consequence, *much of my*

early manuscripts, Scott's letters and more or less valuable documents be-
came rat and roach food. [7] (Italics added.)

One might have some doubts as to the accuracy of this statement (since
Hemingway is once more apologizing for not sending something of a personal nature to an outsider) were it not for the fact that fourteen years earlier, on December 16, 1935, he had written to Fitzgerald from Key West that
he had just found Fitzgerald's long letter to him in which he advised him
about the ending of *A Farewell to Arms.* This clearly corroborates the fact
that Hemingway had some of his early manuscripts and letters in Key West.

The evidence in favor of Hemingway's having left trunks of old manuscripts in Paris for some thirty years outweighs slightly the evidence against
it—the most powerful piece of evidence remaining Mary's and Ernest's
claims to that effect. However, there is valid evidence—if basically negative
evidence—that suggests that the discovery of these trunks may have been a
myth added to Hemingway's already legendary life.

The most tangible evidence against the discovery of the trunks as Mary
described it is the fact that the old employees at the Ritz Hotel who remember Hemingway clearly, and who remember that he often left things at the
Ritz from one year to the next, *do not remember* that he ever left anything
for thirty years. [8] Another factor which militates against the story as told by
Hemingway and Mary is the fact that Ernest apparently never mentioned
the discovery of these papers in his private correspondence, even in his letters to close friends like General Lanham and Harvey Breit.

For instance, Hemingway wrote to Harvey Breit from Paris, while staying at the Ritz, in December 1956, shortly after the papers had supposedly
been discovered, and he does not mention that discovery at all; neither does
he mention it in any subsequent letter to him. Nor does he mention it to
General Lanham, to whom he wrote very long letters full of details about
his personal life. In his letter to Lanham of April 8, 1957, he talks about the
past summer and fall in Spain and Paris, gives many details about his health
but does not mention the trunks or the papers. Mary Hemingway herself,
who wrote to Patrick and his wife on December 27, 1956, from the Ritz,
makes no mention of the trunks in her long and chatty letter; neither does
Hemingway mention the trunks to "Mouse" in any of his letters of that
period. As a matter of fact, I have not found one single mention of the
trunks in the Hemingway correspondence which is at the Kennedy Library,
Princeton University Library, the Beinecke Library, and the Houghton Library.

Finally, it seems somewhat unlikely that Hemingway would have left two
trunks in the Ritz basement before moving to Key West in 1928 instead of
shipping them with the rest of his baggage, especially if he considered them
important enough to instruct the baggagemen at the Ritz to take good care
of them, as they contained important papers. [9] Although Hemingway admittedly had a tendency to leave manuscripts in various places, such as a barn

which burned down in Piggott or at Sloppy Joe's Bar in Key West, it just does not seem quite logical that he would have left these trunks in a hotel where he and Pauline did not even stay after they had given up the apartment in the Rue Férou. Of course, Hemingway was probably a good customer of the Ritz Bar and friendship with bartenders can perhaps lead to trunks stored in a basement.

Other evidence of trunks stored in Paris can be found in the correspondence between Hemingway and Gerald Murphy and between Mary Hemingway and Mr. Mourelet, concierge at the Ritz. On September 20, 1937, Gerald Murphy wrote to Hemingway that he had left at the Elysée Park Hotel, where he was staying, three pieces of luggage belonging to Hemingway to be kept in storage. Attached to the letter was a receipt for the luggage from the concierge of the hotel. What these pieces of luggage were is difficult to determine. There is, of course, a slim chance that they might have been pieces of luggage left by Hemingway in the Murphy's studio, Rue Froidevaux, ten years earlier. Correspondence between the Hemingways and Mr. Mourelet dates back to 1950, and involves a trunk of old clothes and manuscripts, two boxes of books and one box of china, which were to be shipped to Cuba. When these had been left at the Ritz is unclear and it seems that the trunk belonged to Mary: "I think we should insure the books for $200.00 and the China for $100.00. If *my trunk* [italics added] has also been held up, would you insure that and its contents (which are simply personal belongings, old clothes, letters, and manuscripts) for $200.00.[10] One can hardly imagine that, if the trunk had contained Hemingway's early manuscripts, it would only have been insured for $200.00. However, the description of the contents of that trunk comes disturbingly close to the description of Hemingway's forgotten trunks at the Ritz.

Should there have been no trunks full of old manuscripts stored in the Ritz basement for some thirty years, Hemingway's self-dramatization and myth-making, if such it is, would have served several practical purposes. It would have served as a justification for his writing the same sort of thing, and, much worse, that he had only recently violently attacked Arthur Mizener for writing; for destroying in print people whom he had never liked and some he had professed to like; and finally for writing a book he had always claimed that he would write only when he could not write about anything else.

Hemingway had been extremely angered by Mizener's article on Fitzgerald published on January 15, 1951, as evidenced by the letters he wrote to Harvey Breit, Malcolm Cowley and Mizener himself.[11] For instance, on January 17, 1951, he wrote to Breit:

> Just read the piece in *Life*. I wrote him that he was an undertaker; but that piece is straight grave robbing and he sells the body. I will have to see him

some time to see who can do such things . . . . Maybe he's a nice guy. But the *Life* piece is not nice and it has his name on it.

. . . . .

I'd kill a guy for money if times were bad enough, I guess. But I don't think I could do that.

Hemingway kept harping on Mizener's article for a long time in his correspondence with various people. To Mizener himself he wrote, on January 18, 1951: "For your information I would gladly clean sewers for a living, every day, or bounce in a bad whore house or pimp for a living than to sign such an article."

However, when he himself got around to writing on Fitzgerald, barely five or six years after this exhibition of outrage, what he wrote about him was probably more destructive than anything Mizener had written, for he made a fool of Scott and presented him as a total failure as a man, and close to one as a writer. He was clearly aware of it, too, for, in 1957, when *The Atlantic* asked him for an article for their 100th Anniversary number, he wrote a piece on how he had met Scott, but had qualms about sending it once it was done:

I started to write about Scott and how I first met him and how he was; writing it all true and it was tough to write and easy to remember and I thought it was very interesting. But when I read it over I remembered that character writing about his friend Mr. Dylan Thomas and thought people would think I was doing that to Scott and him dead. So I had worked a month on it and finished it good and then put it away and wrote them a story.[12]

There seems to be little doubt that this is what became, with few revisions, the first chapter on Scott in *A Moveable Feast*, for there seems to be no other manuscript of his meeting with Scott. It is interesting to notice that he was still hesitant about these chapters in the fall of 1958, for he contradicts himself in two letters written within three days of each other—of course, it could also be that, depending on his audience, he was assuming a different attitude. On September 18, 1958, he wrote to Buck Lanham that he had done "a book, very good, about early earliest days in Paris, Austria, etc.—the true gen on what everyone has written about and no one knows but me." Three days later, he wrote to Harvey Breit that the book was "*unreadable*" and that he would probably throw it in the waste basket. Hemingway, thus, clearly knew the impact of what he had written, and claiming that he had written it after he had unexpectedly discovered notes taken during his early years in Paris could have been, consciously or not, a way of shirking full responsibility for his merciless portrait of Fitzgerald.

In any case, the discovery of the Ritz Hotel papers gave Hemingway an ideal excuse for writing about his former friends—writing things which he had often said in his private correspondence but that he had never made public property until that day. The discovery of the papers and the claim that they gave him the idea of writing the book lent authenticity to what he wrote and established the purity of his motives. It thus appeared that it was not Hemingway, the bitter and somewhat paranoiac writer who was stabbing at Gertrude Stein, Ford Madox Ford, Fitzgerald, Ernest Walsh, Cheever Dunning and others, but the older Hemingway reporting accurately on what the young Hemingway had seen and felt. It had the strength of documentary evidence; thus no one could question the accuracy of the anecdotes he related, and no one could say that he was revenging himself for what Gertrude Stein had written about him in *The Autobiography of Alice B. Toklas*. His phone call to Hadley, though, certainly establishes the fact that his intentions were not entirely pure.[13] Clearly forgetting his own earlier baiting of Gertrude Stein, he had often claimed, in private correspondence, that he had never attacked her or retaliated after *The Autobiography*. For instance, he wrote to Gingrich on November 16, 1934:

> . . . it goes against my digestion to take shots at anyone who's ever been a friend no matter how lousey they get to be finally. Besides, I've got the gun and it's loaded and I know where the vital spots are and friendship aside there's a certain damned fine feeling of superiority in knowing you can finish anybody off whenever you want to and still not doing it.

Finally, the discovery of the papers gave him the perfect opportunity for writing the book he had often said he would write when he had nothing else to write about, that is, when his genius had dwindled. Without such an excuse, the mere writing of the book would have been an admission to himself and his friends that he had indeed reached the end of his rope as a writer. Angry as ever about critics who wanted to write his biography, he wrote to Malcolm Cowley on May 13, 1951:

> Did it ever occur to any of these premature grave robbers that *when I was through writing books* I might wish to write the story of my life myself if the people concerned were dead so that they would be hurt no more than I would? *Writing it with the evidence to back it up and telling the part few people know about it.* (Italics added.)

Much earlier, just after the publication of Gertrude Stein's memoirs, he had written to Janet Flanner on April 8, 1933: "By Jeeses will write my own memoirs sometimes when I can't write anything else. And they will be funny and accurate and not out to prove a bloody thing". On July 22, 1933, he also wrote to Ezra Pound: "Well gents it will be a big day when write my own bloody memoirs because Papa isn't jealous of anyone (yet) and have a damned rat trap memory and nothing to prove. Also the documents—Il faut toujours garder les paperasses." And to Max Perkins, on July 26: "I'm going to write damned good memoirs when I write them because I'm jealous of no one, have a rat trap memory and the documents. Have plenty to write first though."

It is interesting to note that even before Gertrude Stein had attacked him

Hemingway had intended to use his memoirs as a weapon against those he did not like. For instance, he wrote to Pound on February 2, 1932:

> Listen—did Walsh ever promise you that $2500 prize in writing or only verbally—I saved the letter in which he promised it to me and will use it when I write my own fuckin memoirs which will strive for accuracy. . . . Am not going to write these memoirs until commenced over a period of years that unable to write anything else. Hope will be some time yet. [14]

That he still meant his memoirs, in 1961, to be an attack on some people is made clear by his phone call to Hadley shortly before his death.

Thus, the idea of writing his autobiography certainly did not come to Hemingway as an "epiphany" after the discovery of the Ritz-Hotel papers. It was in fact an idea which he had entertained for a very long time, and, in particular, since the publication of *The Autobiography of Alice B. Toklas*. Moreover, by 1956, many of his contemporaries had also published their memoirs of the early days in Paris, which gave him an added reason for writing his own. Whether or not he truly discovered trunks of old manuscripts in the basement of the Ritz, he could not have found a more convenient reason for writing his memoirs at a time when his creative genius was escaping him. His memories of the old days in Paris, old manuscripts which he had either found in the famed trunks or had always had in his possession, added to his resentments and loyalties, would provide the inspiration he was lacking. Moreover, claiming that these trunks had given him the idea of writing his memoirs would exonerate him from accusations of resentment, or so he probably subconsciously hoped.

If one returns to the assumption that Hemingway left trunks in storage at the Ritz in the late Twenties, it is of course important to attempt to determine at what time he might have done so, as this would influence the possible contents of these trunks. If Hemingway did indeed leave two trunks stored at the Ritz, the most unlikely time for him to have done so, despite Mary's statement, is in 1928 before going to Key West, for he was at that time comfortably settled in an apartment at 6 Rue Férou. Moreover, according to Ernest's letter to Gus Pfeiffer, he already had four trunks stored somewhere in Paris in 1928. This leaves two periods of time when Hemingway would have been likely to store things: after his break up with Hadley and when he and Pauline had to give up the apartment at the Rue Férou.

When Ernest and Hadley separated, Ernest moved into Gerald Murphy's studio in the Rue Froidevaux and Hadley found a room at the Hotel Beauvoir and later an apartment at 35 Rue de Fleurus. It is from that apartment that she wrote Ernest on November 19, 1926, that he could "take over [his] suitcase, etc. They are all piled up in the dining room." However, Ernest kept the apartment of the Rue Notre-Dame-des-Champs until early June 1927 and left a part of his belongings there until he married Pauline. In a tiny little notebook in which he had made a list of the things he needed to do before his marriage to Pauline, he had indicated:

> Sunday
> go to church
> pack letters etc. at 113 ND
> dinner at 6 rue Férou
> tell Marie to arrive with Tonton for 113 packing
> p.m. move things with Tonton and Marie

In 1926 and 1927, therefore, Hemingway's belongings were spread out among four apartments, and it would be a little surprising that he should also have stored things at the Ritz. Moreover, at that time, his connection with the Ritz could only have been slight, for it was still his period of poverty.

Ernest and Pauline clearly left the apartment at the Rue Férou very unwillingly in late December 1929, or probably early January 1930, after the owner had terminated their lease, as evidenced by Hemingway's letter to Maxwell Perkins of September 27, 1929:

> We haven't heard yet is we can stay in this apartment. (Put 3000 dollars into fixing it and improvements on strength of supposedly valid lease). If we are kicked out will store some things and bring others over, probably landing in Cuba and Key West as before sometime in December.

I have not been able to determine where they stored their furniture and belongings between December 1929 and September 1931, when they probably shipped everything to Key West and returned there to settle in the new house.[15] Therefore, the most probable time for Hemingway to have stored trunks at the Ritz would have been in December 1929 or early January 1930; but why would he have done so instead of putting these trunks in storage with the rest of his belongings, of which he had made a cautious inventory with estimated values, probably for insurance purposes, in another small notebook? Moreover, it appears that Hemingway and Pauline did not stay at the Ritz after they had given up the Rue de Férou apartment, or before they settled into it, for that matter.[16]

There is, therefore, a good chance that Hemingway did leave trunks stored in Paris for a time, but it seems unlikely that he left them at the Ritz in the late 1920s as he and Mary later claimed. He possibly left them elsewhere, and they might have been transferred to the Ritz later; whether they stayed at the Ritz until 1956 is also doubtful. Mary's emphasis on the discovery of these trunks in her review of *A Moveable Feast* could well have been intended to exonerate Ernest from accusations of spitefulness in his treatment of fellow authors.

At this juncture, it seems to me that it is virtually impossible to identify specifically the manuscripts which could have been in the trunks. It is well known that Hemingway gave his manuscripts to his friends rather easily.

Even if one could track down every early manuscript which he gave away, it would still be impossible to determine which one could have been left in the trunks, for, as we also know, he had taken some of these early manuscripts to Key West. Actually, it is more than likely that he had some of them with him as early as January 1930 when he was working on *Dealth in the After-noon* at the Nordquist Ranch in Wyoming. At least one passage of the book—the story of the quarrel between two homosexuals in Chapter Six-teen—is clearly rewritten from an earlier manuscript entitled "There is one in Every Town" which descibes the way young Americans become homo-sexuals in Paris. Thus, the closest that I can come—and admittedly it is not very close—is to say that any manuscript of stories or novels written prior to 1930 which is now at the Kennedy Library could possibly have been in the trunks. In them there could also have been letters from friends such as Ezra Pound, sketches of his contemporaries, drafts of letters to his landlord, old bull-fight tickets, programs of exhibitions, etc. Of course, one should not forget to mention the "blue-and-yellow-covered notebooks" described by Mary Hemingway.[17] Twenty-four of the twenty-seven notebooks dating back to the Twenties now at the Kennedy Library could have been in the trunks. Moreover, if there was in the trunks the manuscript of one novel, it had to be the manuscript of *The Sun Also Rises* and not that of *A Farewell to Arms* (however improbable it might seem that Hemingway should have thus left unattended the manuscript of his first and very successful novel). Had this and other manuscripts been at the Ritz as he later claimed, one would expect that rescuing them would have been one of his major preoccu-pations when he "freed" the Ritz just before the liberation of Paris in 1944.

Actually, Hemingway made relatively small use of his early manuscripts in the writing of *A Moveable Feast*. So far, I have been able to find only two instances of borrowing from *The Sun Also Rises*, one from "Big Two-Hearted River"[18] and a few other miscellaneous borrowings from early manuscript fragments.

The passage about Ford Madox Ford cutting Hilaire Belloc was borrowed by Hemingway from the first notebook of *The Sun Also Rises* (p. 13), but it has been very much reworked and integrated with other material. In the notebook Ford was thinly disguised under the name of Braddock. This passage disappeared when Hemingway decided to follow Fitzgerald's advice and lopped off the first fifteen typewritten pages of the manuscript.[19] The passage about the Lost Generation was borrowed from the brown notebook containing the foreword to "The Lost Generation—A Novel" in which Hemingway explains why he decided finally not to call his first novel "The Lost Generation." The original passage, however, was very much reworked for inclusion in *A Moveable Feast* and the overtone of war was a straight addition:

One day last summer Gertrude Stein stopped in a garage in a small town in the Department of Ain to have a valve fixed in her Ford car. The young mechanic who fixed it was very good and quick and skillful. . . .

"Where do you get boys to work like that?" Miss Stein asked the owner of the garage. "I thought you could not get boys to work any more."

"Oh, yes," the garage owner said. "You can get very good boys now. I've taken all of these and trained them myself. It is the ones between 22 and 30 that are no good. C'est un generation perdu [sic]. No one wants them. They are no good. They were spoiled. The young ones, the new ones are all right today."

"But what becomes of the others?"

"Nothing. They know they are no good. C'est un generation perdu." A little hard on them, he added.

The difference between this passage and the version Hemingway published in *A Moveable Feast* is obvious, and there seems to be little need to comment.

Some of the comments which Hemingway makes in *A Moveable Feast* about his learning to write in Paris and the influence of Cézanne on his craft are strongly reminiscent of the deleted passage of "Big Two-Hearted River," which has now been published as "On Writing" in *The Nick Adams Stories*.[20] Although there seems to be no direct textual borrowing, the ideas are similar and the attitude of the writer analysing his own craft and giving clues to his characterization is already present in "On Writing."

Other minor borrowings are from Item 484 in Jo August's directory of the papers at the Kennedy Library. Short passages from these manuscript fragments have been used, and mostly reworked, in *A Moveable Feast*. A good instance is the first paragraph of Item 484 which obviously was the model for the first paragraph of chapter 5, "People of the Seine," in the book. However, it is much more difficult to date these fragments, and there is always a distant possibility that they might have been merely an early draft for *A Moveable Feast*. Another possible borrowing is the headnote for the Fitzgerald section which Philip Young describes as "considerably older than the rest of the manuscript."[21] It does look older, and it certainly is written on a different type of paper, as it has been torn out of a small notebook. However, I have not been able to find among the early notebooks the one from which this small sheet of paper could have been torn out. None of them has a similar format.

An attempt at determining whether the story told by Hemingway and Mary about the trunks of old manuscripts left at the Ritz Hotel in Paris in the Twenties is accurate and at identifying specifically the manuscripts which were in these trunks is an enterprise which meets with many frustrations. Further information on this matter will probably come mostly from personal testimonies—those, however, are unfortunately more and more difficult to gather since some of the people involved are now dead (i.e.

Pauline, Charles Ritz, Leonard Lyons, etc.). At this point, the evidence in favor of the story as told by Hemingway and, especially, Mary is not overwhelmingly convincing, and there is a possibility that the whole thing was a figment of Hemingway's imagination. In any case, whether Hemingway discovered some of his old manuscripts at the Ritz in 1956, or whether he had had them in his possession for a long time before that, he made relatively small use of them in the composition of *A Moveable Feast*. A study of the manuscripts reveals, with little chance of error, that the book was written late in Hemingway's life, and that no major or even minor portion of the book was written in the Twenties. Thus its "stylistic felicities" were not achieved during his youth, but were Hemingway's last achievement. If he actually did discover trunks of old manuscripts, they only served to bring back to memory details he might have forgotten. A study of Hemingway's letters, though, shows that he remembered occurrences rather well, or, at least that he was faithful to his own version of things to the end. A study of the letters is, in fact, more rewarding from the point of view of the composition of *A Moveable Feast* than a study of the old manuscripts, as it is relatively easy to find in them the origin of many of the episodes he relates in the book. At times, his memoirs even appear to be a combination of the gossip and anecdotes he wrote to such friends and acquaintances as Ezra Pound, Charles Scribner, Donald Gallup, Edmund Wilson and others, with the exception, of course, of the beautiful and evocative descriptions of Paris, which are the true strength of the book. But that is another topic.

In any case "a good story is a good story is a good story. . . ." And I should like to close with the following quotation from the Hemingway papers:

> It is not unnatural that the best writers are liars. A major part of their trade is to lie or invent and they will lie when they are drunk, or to themselves, or to strangers. They often lie unconsciously and then remember their lies with deep remorse. It they knew all other writers were liars too it would cheer them up.
>
> Sometimes two of them will lie to a stranger and then they enjoy it without remorse. If they would realize that no stranger is entitled to the truth and that no one knows the truth anyway they would be spared much remorse. . . . Not having done penance I will prepare to write again. [handwritten on the back of that same page]. To start new again I will try to write truly about the early days in Paris.

NOTES

1 See the following: George P. Hunt: "Editor's Note," Mary Hemingway's: "The Making of the Book: A Chronicle and a Memoir," Lewis Galantière's: "There is Never Any End to Paris," Mildred Carr's "The Young Hemingway Looks at Paris, A 'Moveable Feast,' " and Reece Stuart's; "Young, Hungry Hemingway Found Paris a 'Feast.' "

2 Carlos Baker corrected Mary's faulty date in *Ernest Hemingway: A Life Story* (New York: Bantam, 1970) p. 679.

3 A.E. Hotchner: *Papa Hemingway* (New York: Random House, 1955) p. 297.

4 Mary Hemingway: *How It Was* (New York: Alfred A. Knopf, 1976) p. 440.

5 The letters quoted in this article are from the following collections: Hemingway's letter to Gus Pfeiffer, Julien Cornell, Malcolm Cowley and Mizener are from the Kennedy Library; Hemingway's letters to Ezra Pound are from Yale's Beinecke Library; Hemingway's letters to Maxwell Perkins, Buck Lanham, Arnold Gingrich, and Janet Flanner are from Princeton University Library; Hemingway's letters to Harvey Breit are from Harvard's Houghton Library. Mary Hemingway's letters to Mr. Mourelet are at the Kennedy Library.

6 For a good summary of the Hemingway/Seldes quarrel, see Carlos Baker: *A Life Story,* pp. 816-817.

7 Carlos Baker suggests that the "someone" is Pauline.

8 Letter written to the author by Frank Klein, present Managing Director of the Ritz, May 27, 1980: "Malgré tout notre désir de vous être agréable, les livres de mise en garde de 1926 et 1928 ayant été détruits, nous ne pouvons vous renseigner. Les vieux employés se souviennent que Monsieur Hemingway laissait toujours des réserves entre ses voyages mais aucun d'eux ne se rappelle qu'il y ait laissé des objets pendant trente ans."

9 See Mary Hemingway's *How It Was*, p. 440.

10 Mary Hemingway to Mr. Mourelet, April 24, 1950; see also letters from Mary to Mourelet, August 15, 1950 and from Mr. Mourelet to Hemingway, April 4, 1950.

11 Arthur Mizener: "F. Scott Fitzgerald's Tormented Paradise," *Life*, XXX, January 15, 1951, pp. 82-88, 91-94, 96-99.

12 Letter to Harvey Breit, June 16, 1957.

13 See Alice Hunt Sokoloff: *Hadley, The First Mrs. Hemingway* (New York: Dodd, Mead & Company, 1973), p. 101: "The last time that Hadley had heard from Ernest Hemingway was in March, 1961. . . . He wanted to ask her if she could recall the name of someone in Paris during their years together, someone who had not treated the younger writers as he should."

14 Disturbingly, there is no such letter from Ernest Walsh to Hemingway in the collection at the Kennedy Library, at the Beinecke or at Princeton University library.

15 Carlos Baker indicates that Pauline was preparing in Paris to send her furniture to Key West in the spring of 1931, *A Life Story*, p. 284.

16 Hemingway and Pauline stayed at hotels such as the Hotel Foyot (Rue de Tournon), the Crystal Hotel (Rue St. Benoit), and, in particular, the Paris-Dinard, where Pauline stayed in May 1931.

17 These notebooks have been described by Philip Young and Charles Mann in *The Hemingway Manuscripts: An Inventory* and by Jo August in her guide to the Hemingway papers at the Kennedy Library. However, there is no systematic description of them, since both the book and the guide deal with the Hemingway papers at large and do not focus in any particular way on the notebooks. Moreover both of them are incomplete.

18 I am grateful to Bernard Oldsey for having drawn my attention to this particular borrowing.

19 Even before Hemingway decided to cut off the beginning of the novel, Maxwell Perkins had objected to Hemingway's use of the name Belloc, and Hemingway had felt that it was pointless to publish that passage without Belloc's name in it and had decided to delete the whole passage. See letter from Hemingway to Maxwell Perkins, August 21, 1926, and Perkins's letter to Hemingway, May 18, 1926.

20 Ernest Hemingway: *The Nick Adams Stories* (New York: Scribner's, 1972) p. 233-241.

21 Philip Young and Charles Mann: *The Hemingway Manuscripts: An Inventory*, (University Park and London: The Pennsylvania State University Press, 1969) p. 19.

INITIAL EUROPE: 1918 AS A SHAPING ELEMENT
IN HEMINGWAY'S *WELTANSCHAUUNG*

Zvonimir Radeljković

Of the seven Hemingway novels published during his lifetime, four take place in Europe, and only two in the United States. One of these two is *The Torrents of Spring,* his early ironic refutation of Sherwood Anderson's influence. The other is *To Have and Have Not.* In other words, all Hemingway's major novels with the exception of *the Old Man and the Sea* have Europe as their place of action. But what were the effects of his first exposure to the old world, primarily in the context of his unpublished papers? Europe through Paris started Hemingway on his career, although most of his teachers were Americans in Paris. Europe was also the place where he received many shocks, not the least perhaps on July 8, 1918, when he was seriously wounded. Italy, France and Spain, perhaps not in that order, were all at some time his second countries, lands whose culture, civilization and characteristic world-view helped him at least to appreciate his own.

War, to be sure, was perhaps the main European ingredient which Hemingway saw in 1918. War revealed itself to the still idealistic Midwestern boy who dreamed of heroism and saw the enemy as the visiting football team through Paris bombarded by the Big Bertha; through Milan where the munition factory had exploded on the day of his arrival and where he helped carry parts of dead female bodies; and finally through his wound near Fossalta. Although immediately after his arrival at the Red Cross unit he had contributed a Ring Lardnerish humoristic account of war in a Red Cross monthly called, with a slight touch of black humor, *Ciao,* he changed his tone if not his opinion after his wounding. This is how he writes home from the hospital in Milan:

> You know they say there isn't anything funny about this war, and there isn't.
> I wouldn't say that it was hell ... but there have been about eight times when I
> would have welcomed hell, just on a chance that it couldn't come up to the
> phase of war I was experiencing.[1]

In one of his early, until recently unpublished poems (probably written in 1920 or 1921, judging by the Chicago address on it), titled "Killed, Piave 8th July 1918" he continues in this vein imagining himself dead and presenting the grief of a girl who speaks the poem:

> Desire and
> All the sweet pulsing aches
> And gentle hurtings

> That were you,
> Are gone into the sullen dark.
> Now in the night you come unsmiling
> To lie with me
> A dull, cold, rigid bayonet
> On my hot-swollen, throbbing soul. [2]

War is also an agent of destruction in his possibly first prose attempt to analyse the effects of war upon young men, in the unpublished short story "The Mercenaries," probably written in Petoskey in the fall of 1919.[3] In spite of the fact that the story opens in Chicago after the war, the narrator who has the same name as an important character in *A Farewell to Arms,* Rinaldo Rinaldi, discusses with two other characters their respective war experiences and the meaning of courage in war as well as in the postwar world. They also comment on the heroic and amorous exploits of one of them, but the predominant tone of the whole story is the one of despair: the only way out, it seems to these people, is in seeking redemption in new wars because peace seems absurd and senseless.

So it would seem that Hemingway was affected by war in the same or similar way as many other American writers; it appears that he, like Faulkner in *Soldier's Pay* or *Sartoris* or Dos Passos in *Three Soldiers,* portrays the loss of illusions and beliefs of young men and the gradual discovery of evil and tragedy as unavoidable parts of life, American dream notwithstanding. One might claim that Bayard Sartoris from Faulkner's novel *Sartoris* and Krebs from Hemingway's story "Soldier's Home" have a very similar view of the world, since war stands for both of them as the denial of the prewar world in which they grew up, the world of security and complacency which, at least for them, had ceased to exist.

But Hemingway's first European experience contains one other ingredient at least. The first intimations of his view of Europe as not totally defined by war and violence can be seen in a piece of advice which young Hemingway gave to his sister Marcelline immediately after he came back from Italy in 1919. He says:

> ... don't be afraid to taste all the other things in life that aren't here in Oak Park. This life is all right, but there's a whole big world out there full of people who really feel things. They live and love and die with all their feelings. Taste everything, Sis. ... Don't be afraid to try new things just because they *are new.* Sometimes I think we only half live over here. The Italians live all the way.[4]

Europe, in other words, stands in young Hemingway's mind for intensity, for a quality of living never quite reached "back home," for emotional freedom which, it seems, he never felt before then.

His most interesting unpublished short story in that respect is certainly "The Woppian Way," written in the fall of 1919 under the influence and inspiration of his war experience. The main character of the story, which in its very title makes a slur on racial slurs, is a boxer of Italian extraction, an American citizen who had to change his name into Pickles McCarthy in order to have a chance to succeed in professional boxing. Succeed he does—he reaches almost the top rung of the ladder and becomes challenger for the world title—but then he disappears. He emerges again in Italy under his real name, Neroni, as a member of the elité Italian army troups, the Arditti. The story deals predominantly with Neroni's war experiences, but sometimes, through the narrator, one is allowed, as it were, certain perceptions which appear to be common to the narrator and young Hemingway. These perceptions are totally unrelated to war, but function rather as a means of comparing two worlds, the old and the new:

> There's a lot to war beside fighting you know. And every time we would walk in the moonlight down to the trattoria and I'd smell those big purple flowers that mat over the white walls and just ooze perfume into the night, and we'd sit in the little garden with a real stein of pre-war brew before us, and couples walking by, hazy in the moonlight, and maybe up the street a guitar playing A Torno A Sorriento with a kind of hopeful sob in it. [5]

This strangely romantic image of Europe seems to indicate, through some kind of a catalogue of sensory perceptions available to the young soldier in Europe, such as a real stein of pre-war brew, the siluettes of lovers in the moonlight, or the guitar twanging an old and well known folk song full of yearning, that such aspects of life might be completely different or non-existent in America. Europe for Hemingway, apparently, also meant the first contact with an environment different from the surroundings he had been used to, with the kind of feedom in human relationships which did not exist in the Oak Park of his youth. This early story seems to be permeated by "the great American disease," the longing for an experience different from any aspect of American life, which Henry James describes in his short story "Four Meetings" as

> the appetite, morbid and monstruous, for colour and form, for the picturesque and the romantic at any price. . . . We're like travellers in the desert—deprived of water and subject to the terrible mirage, the torment of illusion, of the thirst fever. [6]

This kind of Hemingway's thirst seems to have been quenched, up to a degree at least, during his first exposure to Europe.

But there is still another aspect, almost some kind of a revelation, a kind of change in his world view, triggered by his first stay in Europe. Europe for Hemingway became not only an entity different and separate from America, but also a kind of a touchstone, a yardstick to measure America by. European experience, especially the experience of war, makes his characters aware of many things in America they were not able to see before; it makes them able to differentiate between appearance and reality. This aspect of

the meaning of Europe for young Hemingway can be perhaps most explicitly seen in another unpublished untitled short story written in the same
period in which a character says:

> Jerry and Barney won't be seventeen till next year and they've been out six
> months and Barney got his croce di guerra for that last show on Pasubio. And
> Jerry has a wife in every town in Italy. They're kids and I'm a kid but are we
> like that story? Why Stein I'm a million years old.[7]

The story the characters talk about, which seems to them dated, false and
pathetic, is in fact a sentimental novel for youth, Booth Tarkinton's *Seven-
teen,* published in 1916. Hemingway read the novel in high school and his
mother always thought it was an excellent description of childhood and
youth.[8]

The same attitude in a somewhat different framework can be seen in another early unpublished short story which was probably written at the same
time as "The Woppian Way," the story entitled "Cross Roads, An
Anthology." In its title and structure it clearly shows the influence of Sherwood Anderson and Edgar Lee Masters. It is organized in six short sections,
each bearing the name of a character. Of course, it is a series of portraits depicting inhabitants of a small town in America. Two portraits are especially
interesting. The first one is of a man named Bob White who spent three
days in France during the First World War—and then came the Armistice.
Back home he pretends to be a war hero, very knowledgeable about France.
He has a low opinion of the French, both men and women, since, as he
claims, the men are cowards who refused to fight their own war, and the
women are all ugly. One ought to remember that the epigraph of the Paris
edition of *in our time* and the first New York edition of *In Our Time,* was
also an attempt to mock this type of American chauvinism. It runs:

A GIRL IN CHICAGO: Tell us about the French women, Hank.
                             What are they like?

BILL SMITH: How old are the French women, Hank?

The second portrait distinctly contrasts with the first one. It presents an
Indian, Billy Gilbert, who went to the war as a volunteer, fought very brave-
ly in a Highlander division, and returned home as a legitimate hero. But
when he appears on the streets of his hometown in his Scottish uniform
everybody seems to be amused and slightly disgusted by an Indian in a skirt.
Prejudice and ignorance run deep: the town cannot accept an Indian as a
hero, even more so because his wife abandoned him during his stay in Europe and ran away with another man. So, instead of getting the welcome of a
hero, Billy Gilbert has to leave his hometown in disgrace. As he goes down
the road he whistles a well known Scottish song that says "It's a long way to
Tipperary." [9]

European experience in this fragment acts as a catalyst, as it were. It enables Billy Gilbert to become aware of the ignorance and narrowness of his fellow citizens, who refuse to acknowledge the mere existence of other people, other customs and other mores which can sometimes be radically different from what one has been used to. Europe, in other words, made Billy aware, but, it certainly did not make him happy, not at home.

Hemingway's trip to Europe, to the old continent and the war, exposed him for the first time to violence on a large scale. This experience doubtlessly contributed to the attitude toward war which appears in everything he ever wrote, from his great novels to journalism. He had discovered at an early age that modern war, for the simple reason of being mechanical, of being fought by a machine consisting of innumerable interchangeable parts, cannot be glorious any longer. But Europe also had other functions which can be seen in his earliest postwar writings: it helped him discover hypocrisy in manners and morals which was characteristic of the environment he grew up in, of Oak Park. It helped him shed a post-Puritan, neo-Victorian skin, and look through his own eyes upon the modern world. It also had a liberating effect upon his senses: for the first time, as it were, he began using all his sensuous capacity. In this way he started to feel as an artist, to feel "what you really felt, rather than what you were supposed to feel." [10] Hemingway's initial exposure to Europe certainly contributed to all the books he was going to write later, books that he himself described, without vanity, as "truer than if they had really happened, and after you are finished reading one you will feel that all that happened to you and afterwards it all belongs to you: the good and the bad, the ecstasy, the remorse and sorrow, the people and the places and how the weather was." [11]

NOTES

1 Quoted in Marcelline Hemingway Sanford, *At the Hemingways: A Family Portrait* (Boston; Little, Brown, 1962), pp. 166-167.

2 Catalogued under No. 534 in the Hemingway Collection of the John F. Kennedy Library in Boston. Published in *Ernest Hemingway: 88 Poems.* ed. Nicholas Gerogiannis (N.Y.: Harcourt Brace Jovanovich/Bruccoli Clark, 1979), p. 35.

3 Typescript of the short story "The Mercenaries", 12 pages, catalogued under No. 572 in the Hemingway Collection of the Kennedy Library.

4 M. Hemingway Sanford, *op. cit.,* p. 184.

5 Manuscript of the short story "The Woppian Way", catalogued under No. 843 in the Hemingway Collection of the Kennedy Library, pp. 6-7.

6 Henry James, "Four Meetings", *The Portable Henry James* (N.Y.: Viking Press, 1968), pp. 47-48.

7 Typescript of the untitled short story catalogued under No. 531 in the Hemingway Collection of the Kennedy Library.

8 M. Hemingway Sanford, *op. cit.,* p. 148.

9 Typescript of the short story "Cross Roads, An Anthology", catalogued under No. 347 in the Hemingway Collection of the Kennedy Library.

10 Ernest Hemingway, *Death in the Afternoon* (N.Y.: Scribner's, 1971), p. 2.
11 Ernest Hemingway, "Old Newsman Writes: A Letter from Cuba", *Esquire,*
    December 1934. Reprinted in *By-Line,* ed. by William White, (Penguin, 1970),
    p. 181.

HEMINGWAY PAPERS, OCCASIONAL REMARKS

Philip Young

"Few Americans had a greater impact on the emotions and attitudes of the American people than Ernest Hemingway. From his first emergence as one of the bright literary stars in Paris during the 20s—as a chronicler of the 'lost generation,' which he was to immortalize—he almost single-handedly transformed the literature and the way of thought of men and women in every country in the world."

Those sentences make up the opening paragraph of a four-paragraph tribute to Hemingway which appeared in a special issue of the *Mark Twain Journal* for Summer, 1962. They were signed by John F. Kennedy, and though a rigorous textual analysis would probably not support me, I would like to think he wrote them. I do not think he wrote the other paragraphs, which read like the work of a subordinate (very) who had located the subject in a reference book. The President of course knew quite enough about the writer to make a statement. As we all know, seven years earlier in his *Profiles In Courage* he had thought of him at the first mention of the word "courage. 'Grace under pressure,' Ernest Hemingway defined it." As not everyone knows, though Theodore Sorensen passed it along, Kennedy once added that "grace under pressure . . . also described a girl he knew by that name."

Kennedy and Hemingway. Back when I was getting ready to bring out a *Reconsideration* of the writer, I was struck with similarities between two of my favorite people, both so suddenly and violently gone. Both were serious, realistic, witty men, who aimed for the top and made it. Both were great readers, both men of style, both students of courage who drew portraits of it. Curiously parallel were their grievous injuries, illnesses, and brushes with death. Knowing a little of the author's admiration for the President, I wrote Arthur Schlesinger, Jr., to ask if Kennedy had perhaps not felt some kind of affinity with Hemingway. Yes indeed, was the friendly response. Schlesinger, who was just finishing his book on Kennedy, said that he "obviously felt an affinity of some sort" with the author. Although when "I got to know him well," he added, the President had pretty much quit reading fiction, "he appeared to have read most of Hemingway at one time or another," and was a "great admirer." He recalled how distressed Kennedy was by the writer's death, and how touched he had been by the message received from the Mayo Clinic at the time of the inauguration. *A Thousand Days* says the same things, and its single epigraph is a passage we know that begins "The world breaks everyone. . . ." Kennedy believed that the health of society related to the health of the arts, which is chiefly why so many artists, including Hemingway, were invited to his inaugural. I don't remember that any professors were asked. But for the present occasion it might be noted that when the White House library was, in Sorensen's words, "restocked and restored with the best in American literature," two critical studies of Hemingway showed up in the acquisitions.

It would be unwise to attempt an extended account of my own relationship with John F. Kennedy. (My mother used to push me in a baby carriage to the neighborhood grocer's in Brookline, and only long afterward realized that the infant perambulated there by Rose Kennedy—recognized by all as Honey Fitz's daughter—had become our senator, then our chief executive. Though the Youngs lived adjacent to the Kennedys—they at 83 Beals Street—we did not know them; like so many in that town, they were Democrats.) But a different sort of connection might be briefly invoked. On or about February 3, 1968, Charley Mann received a note from Mary Hemingway which read:

> By chance I spoke a moment tonight with Robert Kennedy, told him what you and Philip Y. are doing. He appeared very pleased, and said whenever the inventory was ready, he would like very much to have a copy of it.
>
> This is not to harrass or hurry you; only to suggest that the original catalog—or listing or whatever you prefer to call it—have another copy made, not waiting for Philip's printed thing for libraries. . . .

On the back of the envelope she wrote "P. S. We should make one for Mrs. Kennedy too."

February 3, 1968, was the day Senator Kennedy opened his presidential campaign in Concord, N. H. Charley and I were at that point far from ready, but thought it might become us anyway to hurry, and before long we sent Mary copies of a substantial listing. Neither of us recalls what happened next, but by then R. F. K. was well along the trail on which he died in June. In the aftermath of yet another catastrophe we asked nothing, and suppose he never saw what we put together for him. (Asked about this in the Hemingway Room at the time of the dedication, Mrs. Onassis said she does not think she ever saw it either.)

It is hard to think of a time when a rapprochement between the arts and the White House seemed more real than during the Kennedy administration—a sense of rapport, of which the present ceremony is a pointed reminder. It is precisely the ceremonial aspect of all this that attracts me. Similarly it is the remarkable existence and bringing-together of the Papers, more than the use to which they can be put, which I find exciting. But I think we should be mindful, in the presence of such treasure, that if the author had had his way—at least as he once expressed it thirty years ago—we would all be somewhere else today, and the Papers would be nowhere. Posterity,

Hemingway wrote Arthur Mizener in 1950, can take care of herself. What he figured was "to have all my papers and uncompleted Mss. burned when I am buried. I don't want that sort of shit to go on. . . ." It is not specified in the letter what sort that might be, yet I do suspect that the activities we are engaged in would qualify. Nor do I believe that this sentiment of the author's was aberrant or fleeting. It fit his wish—as he expressed it, anyway—that attention would focus exclusively on his published work, not its creator. Also the belief that by issuing a sort of edict he could forever prohibit publication of his letters.

But surely it had been an awful loss if all this paper had gone up in smoke. When I consider the scope and profundity of the universal debt owed the author's widow, I am most impressed by the number of situations in which she must have had to weigh her sense of the writer's wishes against other interests, such as the public. It is not just the enormous energy and effort she has expended, or the skill and judgment with which she has managed things, but the moral quandries she must have endured (so I imagine it) and have had to resolve. We have long honored Max Brod for violating the wishes of his friend Kafka, and issuing posthumously the uncompleted work on which much of a great reputation rests. But Mary H. was not just a friend.

The thought that led to the permanent repository of so much cherished wealth, furthermore, was inspired. What is awkward is the matter of one's own contribution to the program. I first thought it was to be occasional and the truth is that I have not, as advertised, "utilized the Papers in recent years." (It's been over a decade since I glimpsed them, and I never so much "used" as identified, listed and simply read.) Moreover, as some of you know, I have subsequently passed along such thoughts as I could summon up at meetings of this sort in Texas, Oregon, Idaho, Pennsylvania, Alabama, and Florida. The cupboard is very close to bare, and only after some poking around have I managed to locate in its recesses three bits of business commenced yet unfinished. These are, first, an updated report to stockholders in the Hemingway Industry, and, second, a bulletin on the recent fortunes and misfortunes of a book called *The Nick Adams Stories*, which grew out of the Papers. Last there is what may be a final thought on the situation which once nearly stopped the speaker before he ever got started in these affairs.

That story, with which I begin, has been a long time ending—particularly as new insights have appeared. I told it many years ago: the epistolary argument between author and critic, his strong objection to publishing his biography, which critic did not proposé to write, and to a psychological analysis of his work—hence him, which I would attempt. To that narrative I brought all the understanding that I possessed. But I never did truly comprehend Hemingway's fear of what I was doing: most especially his warning (which to be honest I did not believe) that I could put him absolutely out of commission as a writer. All this had come to a head in late May of 1952. But one day long after, while looking for manuscript in a closet at Mary's, I came across several letters he'd written me back then and hadn't mailed. One of them, dated the 27th, is unfinished but representative. In it the author warns that by publishing my book I was about to "damage him, his wife and his children . . . gratuitously and without necessity." I was, he wrote, "at temporary liberty to attempt to destroy me as a writer. . . . "

I wished no such freedom, but since I had written about nothing Hemingway had not himself written about, whence such terrible power? In the context of the letter, it clearly related to the importance I placed on his wounding in Italy in the first World War. He said that in view of all the other wounds he had suffered, many of which he recapitulated, it seemed "silly" that his writing "should have been the result of a wound which was not my first. It was the worst. . . ."

It was also the only meaningful one, as far as his fiction went, and all I was doing was underlining and elucidating the significance he ascribed to it. A piece of a puzzle was missing, and in 1977—a full quarter century later—it turned up. Actually it had been resting in a letter I read that year, which Hemingway had written to Malcolm Cowley back in 1948, in connection with the latter's biographical piece on the former, forthcoming in *Life*. Published in an auction catalog, it is dated October 25th, and reads in part

> . . . look, Malcolm, if you want to do me a favour only put in about Italy . . . that I was wounded on such and such a day . . . had such and such decorations. . . and leave out everything else . . . As you must know from A Farewell to Arms and from In Another Country and A Way You'll Never Be (two uninvented stories) Italy and that part means more to me than I can ever write. I was in very bad trouble there and if you write anything about it *somebody will start digging around and I will*, eventually, *be in bad trouble again*. . . . I was hurt very badly; in the body, mind and spirit and also morally . . . hurt bad all the way through and I was *really spooked* at the end. (Emphasis added.)

As it happens, I had just that summer (in a doctoral dissertation) finished digging around in exactly that area of the writer's *fiction*, pointing out how much "Italy and that part" meant to him and his work. But beyond the well known fact that he like his protagonists had himself been wounded there, all I had to go on was what he had chosen to publish. As I now understand it, what he feared, when I came to his attention three years after he wrote Cowley about this, was that I was digging around in that area of the writer's *life*, and gone into his bad trouble during that period instead of the protagonist's. Then, I imagine, he was afraid that reading all about how it had been, and knowing others were doing the same, would resurrect the demons to spook and incapacitate once more. This was an investigation I never even thought of making, would not have known how to undertake, and would have found distasteful anyway. Biographical details would have been, as he said, gratuitous and unnecessary. Whether they could or would have done the damage he worried about, no one can say. We can only respect his apprehensions, and turn to less painful matters.

I have in mind what are now called "Hemingway Studies"—to me a self-conscious, heavy-handed, and complacent term, which effectively connotes the academic institutionalization of a literary subject. Some time ago, I reported on the considerable growth in this "field." Bemused by it, I thought now to review its history quickly, to extend the survey of productivity into the 70s, and to inquire into its meaning.

We begin by observing that in Lewis Leary's *Articles in American Literature, 1900-1950,* Hemingway titles take up 2¼ pages. (For purposes of comparison, Faulkner fills 3⅓, and to broaden it: Hawthorne and Melville get 7 each, Emerson and James 9, Mark Twain 12, Whitman 12½, and Poe 13½.) One notes that the first Hemingway item appears in 1923: "Hemingway: a Portrait," by Gertrude Stein. (The second, 1925, was Burton Rascoe's and the third, 1926, Scott Fitzgerald's.) By 1950, 91 articles had appeared, for an average of 3 + per annum since the start. It might also be remarked that "serious" Hemingway criticism appears to have begun in the Thirties with J. Kashkeen, John Peale Bishop, and Edmund Wilson, and continued in the Forties with Malcolm Cowley, Robert Penn Warren, and Alfred Kazin out front. Mass production did not get under way until the Fifties, when (working now from the annual *MLA International Bibliography*) the average number of publications per year jumps to 16 +. (In erratic fashion, from a yearly low of 8 to a high of 31; Faulkner's average was 38.) Book-length studies began to appear in 1952, and if anyone was watching it must have looked as though by the end of the decade, at the latest, the important things had been said, and Hemingway Studies must decline before they had achieved that title.

What of course happened instead is that the rate of production in the Sixties better than doubled to an annual average of 42 + entries. (Again spasmodically distributed, from a low of 18 in 1960 to 53 the next year and higher in '69.) And then in the Seventies, with the last year not yet reported, the rate nearly doubled once more to an average of almost 81 items. (Output was also steadier; the championship season was 1974 with a score of 98. And if some of these things are but notes, others are books: "It all evens up"—as, after a few drinks, Nick Adams once remarked.)

The question, I take it, is obvious: whence this snowballing activity? And so, I suppose, is part of the answer: it is a product of the academic situation. Currently, not always. Hemingway criticism used to issue from as far outside collegial walls as it does now from within. (Not one of the pre-1950 names I mentioned strikes us as essentially professorial, though I could have added Oscar Cargill's.) But in three decades things have reversed, as the cloistered pressure to "publish" steeply mounted. Add to this the sharp increase in the number of individuals suddenly belonging to the trade and newly subject to its demands. Hemingway Studies are one result.

Add to this in turn what happens when the study of a literary figure becomes what we now call an Industry. Such a business operates by its own laws. Production, for example, stimulates production. One piece on the now-famous dialogue in "A Clean, Well-Lighted Place"—did the writer get the waiters mixed up?—has spawned twenty others. (With more on the way, though I do believe that David Kerner very recently demonstrated that it was not Hemingway who was confused: Scribner's ought to put the text back the way they had it, and not worry about the cost.) Production creates new opportunities. To chose an obscure one, there is now a little literature on baseball in *The Old Man and The Sea:* what's to be said about that? Another industrial law, as I observed it some time ago, is that the more that's written on a subject the more significant the subject seems, and the more significant it seems the more secondary (tertiary) will be the matters that seem worth going into. For a sobering experience, skim the bibliographies and see how much more important and comprehensive the Hemingway titles become as you move backward in time. Things badly needed a boost when the Papers began to become available for research. Someone with a better prognosticatory record might estimate how long this will keep the ship afloat.

None of this, however, really accounts for the fact that the boom in Hemingway production—like that in Faulkner Studies—has exceeded the general increase in productivity. It was a decade ago that William White announced that the five American writers who had attracted most attention in print were Hawthorne, Melville, James, Faulkner, and Hemingway. The question becomes: why Hemingway? Why should he have overtaken Whitman, Twain, Emerson, and Poe? Faulkner does not surprise me. For one thing, I remember Hemingway's telling Cowley that if he had Faulkner's talent "I would outwrite him 50 to 1." For another, Faulkner presents—like Melville and James—problems and complexities (and, like Hawthorne, ambiguities) that Hemingway by and large does not. One might think that our man offered less to write about. And what, exactly, does all this attention mean? That he is a more important writer than Whitman or Emerson? (And if so, why?)

I do not personally think we have that in mind. In considering alternative explanations, one thing that occurs is that if challenges offered by "difficult" writers invite some they put off others. Access to Hemingway is relatively easy. He has never given middlebrow readers any great trouble, has never appealed to highbrows alone if at all, was never cultish or modish or avant-garde in a bewildering way or a secret prized by an intelligentsia. For over a half-century, people who read fiction have enjoyed reading him. A few go on to study, and a few of these stay to write. His academic popularity, in other words, may not differ in kind from his general popularity. Though they may be detained by deeper and subtler qualities, who is to say that his scholars are not initially drawn by the same ones that attract the reading public? If you are going to work on something, who says you can't like it?

Lots of people—or so, once upon a time, it seemed. You couldn't, for example, get credit for reading anything like *A Farewell To Arms* when I was an undergraduate. The idea was that you read it on your own. Advanced academic work, for the most part, was (is?) precisely what you would not do on your own: the dissertation on Lanier's prosody, Thoreau's reputation in Italy. Past that, it looks as if the profession, having insisted on publication, was forced to admit subjects that may be undertaken with pleasure.

Practically anyone can speculate on the causes of a long bull market. It is more likely that I can contribute something by turning finally to an announcement of second thoughts on a matter where I have been taken severely to task. This reference is to a volume called *The Nick Adams Stories,* 1972, which I gather is widely read. I accept certain responsibilities for it. The original idea of the book was mine, the ordering of the stories is essentially mine, and so, aside from some of the fragments, is the selection of the stories. Likewise a trivial Preface, which replaces a more substantial introduction to the book that, as it turned out, Scribner's did not want. (Since it explained some things about the work, I hurried to get it in print elsewhere [*Novel*, Fall, 1972]; it was reprinted in Jackson Benson's collection of essays on Hemingway's stories, 1975.) Thus in the book there is no mention of a problem I had wrestled for a long time: where in Nick's chronology to put two tales, "The End of Something" and the related "Three-Day Blow." It was to these stories that the banished introduction referred when it admitted that "there isn't any completely satisfactory way to arrange them all, as readers are going to discover when they confront Nick as an adolescent veteran of the great war." The problem has not gone away.

For a long time it had not seemed to exist. I had thought of Nick in these narratives as an adolescent only; clearly they came before the war. Then in 1966 I learned from Constance Montgomery's *Hemingway In Michigan* that they had grown directly out of events in the author's life that occurred during the summer following his return from Italy. I already knew from *At The Hemingways*, his sister Marcelline's book, that a full year later, when he was almost 21, Ernest seemed to her about sixteen. In writing the stories, was he seeing himself as Nick at the time of the events, boyish as he seems, and thus—"most disconcertingly," as I put it—thinking of him as a veteran? When I came to put together the book, I explained the problem in a letter to Charlie Scribner. The circumstances of the stories—as well as of the newly found "Summer People"—belonged to the author's first postwar summer; his persona seemed distinctly prewar. By this time, Carlos Baker's biography had verified and expanded on Montgomery; Charles Scribner consulted his copy, confirmed the biographical data, and that apparently decided the matter. In the book, the stories come after the war—which is where I had with misgivings placed them. I say "apparently": it was about this time that I was dismissed from the project along with my introduction. With this, much of my interest in it dissipated, but I did observe and report on its initial reception, which was mixed. I also remarked that later and more considered responses in the journals would outweigh the first ones, and for the present occasion I examined four "essay-reviews" of the book, which are unfavorable.

Essentially it is the ordering of the stories which is causing trouble for the book's critics. Douglas Wilson (*Western Humanities Review*, Fall, 1973) objects first that the volume contains no statement of what constitutes a Nick Adams story; thus tales are included in which he is not named, and others excluded where he may *be* the "nameless hero." Wilson wants to make Harold Krebs of Oklahoma (which he has Kansas) Nick Adams of Michigan, and he calls another item "in the truest sense, a Nick Adams story" because of a character in it named Horace. (Actually Hemingway used names like Harold and Horace to disqualify them.) But Wilson objects even more to the chronological placement of the stories, and concludes that "nothing . . . is really gained by rearranging" them. He does not explain what the previous arrangement was, or where the new materials go. Robert M. Davis (*Southern Humanities Review*, Spring, 1973) wants them rearranged in the order of composition. (He also wants "Cross-Country Snow" to appear before "Big Two-Hearted River," which would make Nick a married man and presumably a father on that fishing trip.) More emphatically he wants "The Three-Day Blow" put before the war—chiefly because of some conversation in it about the trade of a ballplayer named Heinie Zimmerman to the New York Giants, which occurred in 1916. Most of all he would like to bench the present writer: father of "errors likely to plague a whole generation of students."

So would Bernard F. Rodgers, Jr. (*Fitzgerald/Hemingway Annual, 1974*), who deplores my having "dominated," so he alleges, and "distorted Hemingway scholarship" with a biographical emphasis. One was right in 1952, he says, in putting "Three-Day Blow" and its companion piece before the war: look at Heinie Zimmerman. Look at him a third time, says Stuart L. Burns (*Arizona Quarterly*, Spring, 1977) without mentioning previous observers. But it turns out it's Burns who must be watched. First he thinks the book is a good idea—for quite mistaken reasons and even though a "logical chronology" for the stories is in his view "impossible." Then, having got the year of the author's birth wrong, he appears to attempt what can't be done by figuring Nick's age along the way on the assumption it is the same as Hemingway's (in which case forget Heinie Zimmerman). Finally, as if a chronological ordering did not turn out to be profoundly thematic, he concludes that a thematic arrangement would be best. He is full of questions which a quick reading of the book's deflected introduction (by this time long in print and reprinted) would have answered. Not one of these people profitted from it.

Perhaps this one may benefit from them—if only to concede that the decision on where to put "The End of Something," "The Three-Day Blow," and very likely "Summer People" probably went the wrong way. I would now call these stories dysynchronous, in that Hemingway did not adjust the time of his own fictionalized experience to that of the world's. (The history of the N. Y. Giants, for instance.) Put before the war, I still think the stories anachronous as well: as yet unknown were the rum-runners mentioned in "Summer People"; unless Nick had been in Italy I don't believe he would have planned, as he had, on taking Marge there. As I said before, there is no completely satisfactory place for these stories. But presenting them before the war would have caused less trouble. It would also have fit the fact that the writer was probably seeing himself in them as a prewar protagonist exposed to postwar events—which would indeed have better suited the younger character.

But if I am to end with second thoughts, better they should deal with that remark of Hemingway's about the destruction of his papers at his death. I do imagine that it satisfied him to think that all this material would go to eternity in silence. I suppose the idea of strangers or even friends poring over it would have been displeasing. On the other hand I have a hunch that if he had known about, and had a chance to think about, the honor his widow and the Kennedys have paid him, he would have come privately to rejoice in it. It is evident that the personal attention he tried to avoid in life he also sought. In middle age, anyway, he not only welcomed praise and reassurance but had continual need of them. In his last recorded literary conversation, what struck Leslie Fiedler was "his fear that he had done nothing of lasting worth. . . ." Praise and reassurance on that occasion would have been useless. But it would be hard to dismiss the tribute of the clean, well-lighted place that has been permanently established for him. Or to wish it away.